Praise for Th Bucket Plan

"Our bodies are a temple for the Holy Spirit, and my 'Temple' was a mess. Overweight, out of shape, and spiritually tired, J.T. brought a new and spiritually sound program to the table and it changed my life."

Bob Burns
Missions Pastor, Bayside Church
of Safety Harbor, Florida

"Finally, a program that does not require you to be a scientist, nutritionist, personal trainer or executive chef in order to see results. J.T.'s Empty Your Bucket Program equips everyday people with the necessary tools to make real, long-lasting change in their lives. Body transformation, mental clarity and increased productivity will make you wonder why J.T. waited so long to share his program!"

Rev. Steve Baran
President, National Christian Counselors
Association

"The Empty Your Bucket Plan will change the way you look at nutrition and exercise forever. This program is highly effective and sustainable no matter where your starting point may be. Personally, it has enabled me to make lasting changes for the first time in my life. J.T. is a master motivator and has helped many people improve their lives in a drastic way. This book and J.T.'s proven methods will change your life forever!"

Jason Ferrill
Conference Coordinator, National Christian Counselors Association

"J.T. gets it! He understands the value of honoring God through physical fitness and using exercise as a vehicle to help others move closer to Him. Take advantage of his incredible coaching expertise and read Empty Your Bucket today."

Mollie Yoder
Director of Memberships, Pocket Testament

"Empty your Bucket Plan has changed our life. This plan provided us with the knowledge and understanding of how to not only become healthy, but to have longevity. J.T.'s philosophy on foods provides his readers with a holistic approach to becoming in charge of their own health. My husband Joel went from having high cholesterol, high blood pressure, and being pre-diabetic to having normal blood work for the first time in years. This plan has been a true blessing to my family and me."

Wendy Berry
Professor of Human Performance and Sport Studies, Southeastern University

"J.T. provides valuable insight and wisdom on how to make The Empty Your Bucket Plan a lifestyle, not a diet. It is evident that J.T. has the formula for teaching individuals how to eat in such a way that promotes health and have a greater understanding of the impact foods can have on their life. I highly recommend that people start the Empty your Bucket Plan and regain their wellbeing."

Linette Rivera, M.D.
Endocrinologist, Bella Mia Medical Aesthetics and Laser Institute

The Empty Your Bucket Plan

Strengthening The Mind, Body and Spirit

By

J.T. Tapias

Disclaimer

–

May this book encourage you and guide you on your journey to strengthening your mind, body, and spirit. This book has been on my mind for 17 years. To be completely candid with you, I was intimidated in the beginning of my journey to write a book period—let alone a book on nutrition—even though I have seen incredible (and sustainable) results in members' lives.

I am glad I was patient, because this journey has not only been about nutrition and fitness but a personal transformation in my mind, body, and spirit. I've encountered frustration, temporary defeat, anger, self-pity and an array of challenges that have made me stronger and expanded my faith and relationship with my Lord and Savior Jesus Christ.

I believe resistance in our lives—very much like weight training—is there to strengthen us all. I hope that you apply and live out these principles. They have the potential to make you a stronger, more confident and healthier image-bearer of Christ.

Table Of Contents

Acknowledgements

J.T. would like to thank...

I thank God who had grace over my life and deposited a seed of faith in me, which in turn allowed me to believe in Jesus' sacrificial death on the cross for the forgiveness of my sins. Without this incredible miracle in my life, you would not be reading this book right now. God repurposed my talents in the fitness and nutrition realm that I used for superficial reasons and turned it around and used it for His glory.

I'd like to thank my wife, Ana Maria Tapias, and my daughter Saramia, for motivating, loving, and supporting me in all I do. I've been encouraged to write this book after seeing so many clients in our gym (and all across the world) change in positive ways.

Thank you from the bottom of my heart for believing in this amazing process called, "The Empty Your Bucket Plan."

Introduction

There is a direct connection between our mental, physical, and spiritual health. When we are physically fit and eating a healthy diet, our mind is clear; and this gives us the ability to embrace God. When we feel fantastic and look great, we find ourselves in a unique position to serve and connect with God. However, if we are overweight, sick, or tired, our energy levels are going to be low. Our mindset will be off, and we will tire quickly. We may even find ourselves complaining or consumed with self-pity.

When we become healthy, we will have a level of enthusiasm that is contagious. Other people will notice there is something different about us when we are vibrant and full of energy. Best of all, we can use our lives to exemplify God in a tangible way.

As I am writing this book, the 2018 World Cup is going on. Every other interview I see with these elite athletes has a pretty noticeable common denominator: they all seem to speak about God. A significant component of physical training for these athletes is mental grit. The discipline that is required to take our bodies to another level allows us to understand—if only for a brief moment—the immensity of God's strength and grace. Each of us has been given a physical body to travel through this journey called life. The stronger our physical body is, the better we can serve others. When we fully embrace this concept without vanity or arrogance, it allows us to resemble God's strength; and we find ourselves in a position to lead others to God.

We do not often think of the connection between physical fitness and how God uses us. Recently I had the great opportunity to travel to Israel. As I traveled from Nazareth to Jerusalem, I was amazed to see the rough desert terrain that men and women during biblical times had to cross on foot. I could not stop thinking of the mental, physical, and spiritual strength and commitment it would take to make this journey.

On a map, the straight-line distance from Nazareth to Jerusalem appears to be about 63 miles. However, the actual walking distance would be more on the order of 68 miles. The average adult walking pace is about four miles per hour, so this journey would take at least 17 hours or more. It is hard to sustain a speed of four mph for more than a few hours, so individuals in biblical times would not have achieved this if they were not in tip-top shape.

I hope this book will inspire you to take your physical health to new levels of vibrancy that will help you achieve new spiritual heights.

This book is broken into three specific parts. First, I would like to share with you my personal story of redemption through Jesus Christ and how God used this unique physical platform that helped change my life.

In the second section of the book, I share the details of Temperament Theory and how identifying our God-given temperament can allow us to thrive in all areas of life.

In the last section, I will show you how to implement the Empty Your Bucket Plan and how to make it a sustainable part of your life.

I hope this book will inspire you to take your physical health to new levels of vibrancy that will help you achieve new spiritual heights.

Chapter 1
My Personal Story

I'm originally from Medellin, Colombia. When I was just one year old, I came to the United States with my mother and sister. We had taken a plane into Panama, and from there we took a boat. About halfway through the journey, a storm came out of nowhere. The engine went out near the Bermuda Triangle, and we were in the open ocean for close to three hours. Finally, the captain managed to get the engine going again, and we arrived on the shores of Miami.

I grew up in a third generation Mafia family that was involved in the drug trade. In the early eighties, the Colombian cartels started bringing cocaine into the United States. Each cartel had groups of employees called cells, who were in charge of distributing drugs. They would pick up drugs and distribute the drugs. They were also in charge of specific areas.

Now when we came to the United States, my mom was very innocent—she had grown up around the drug business but was never directly involved in it herself. However, my mother had to figure out a way to make ends meet with two young kids. She worked in a nightclub.

A lot of drug dealers and high rollers would come into the nightclub, spending money on drinks and partying.

My mother was a very attractive, talented woman, but she did not speak English. Some of the men that frequented the club were Colombian. Once they found out she was raising two kids on her own, they felt sorry for her and wanted to help her out.

One evening, a man at the club approached my mother and offered her the opportunity to bring in more income by hiding some money for them. My mother knew from her upbringing that drug dealers have a lot of cash, but the money could not be legitimately placed in the bank. As a result, often those involved in the drug trade would use *calletas* or underground house banks to keep their money safe.

My mother agreed and held on to the money for the man. She handled this job well, and soon a man would stop by our house once or twice a week with bags filled with cash. My mother's job was to count the money and then sort it into small brown bags. I remember there were times that the cash-filled bags filled the entire closet.

After the money was counted, my mother wasn't allowed to go in the closet for any reason. Later in the week, someone would stop by to pick up the money or to drop off even more.

We were a humble family that lived in a not so affluent side of town, so this worked well and did not raise suspicion with others. My mother was paid on a monthly basis so that she wouldn't leave the house.

As my mother continued counting and storing money for those in the drug trade, she rose through the ranks from 1982 to 1992. We were able to get a bigger home and even started to live a luxurious life. My sister and I both went to private schools. At Christmas, there were so many presents that I could barely see the Christmas tree.

At the same time, this was also a very chaotic time. The police were constantly raiding our home. It became part of our lives and caused us to live in a state of fear and anxiety. In 1992, this lifestyle came to an end when my mother was indicted—meaning she was criminally charged—for her involvement in the drug trade. She found out that she could possibly go to jail for up to twenty-five years. To avoid these legal charges, my mother decided to leave the country. We left the United States and went back to Colombia.

When we arrived there, a war was going on. Pablo Escobar was being prosecuted by four different agencies including the KGB, the CIA, Interpol, and a paramilitary organization called Los Pepes.

When we went back to Colombia, my mother continued working in the drug trade. I know you'd have thought she would have learned her lesson, but when you're in this type of business, you can't just quit. She reconnected with drug dealers and continued doing the same thing.

We stayed in Colombia for about four years before things got really bad there. Finally, as violence continued to escalate in the country, we left when I was 14 years old. My sister went to Italy, and I came back to the United States. My mother went to Europe.

I found myself homeless in the streets of New York City. I vividly remember the first night that I didn't have a place to go. It was scary, but at the same time, it was also an adventure.

Thankfully, it was summertime in New York, so it wasn't too cold to sleep outside. I ended up sleeping at Flushing Meadow Park, which is a place where they play the U.S. Open. Because it's a park, a lot of different activities take place there.

One day, I woke up to the sound of footsteps. Some people were walking into the park, and their voices woke me while I was sleeping on a bench. It was a group of kids around my age. I stayed on the bench and kept to myself and acted like I had just gotten there.

A man named Pasqual called me over and said, "Do you want to help us out? We're missing a player."

He had this funny accent. Right away I agreed to play. I had a pair of shorts with holes in them and some old sneakers. I looked nothing like a soccer player, but I jumped on the field to play. I had played soccer before in Colombia many times, and I was actually pretty good.

When I played soccer that day for about 90 minutes, I was so happy. I felt like I belonged. I scored two of the winning goals. I had clarity for the first time in my life. Once I knew how it felt to win, I wanted to do it over and over again.

I found out that Pasqual was the coach. He discovered my living situation and made arrangements with some of the teammates so that I could stay in their house during the week. I would then stay at one home for a few nights, and then I'd go to another home for a few nights, then move on to another.

For those 14 months, whenever I was hungry, I was too embarrassed to ask the person that I was staying with for food. Quite often I would wander into Chinese restaurants in search of food.

I would ask if I could clean the bathrooms or do some work in exchange for a little box of rice to make it through the day. If I was paid, I would use the money to buy a soft drink that had, like, six or seven hundred calories. I would just drink one of those, and that was all I would have all day.

Those were challenging times. But it was also when I developed mental grit. From that point on, I started to appreciate things a lot more. I had never been in circumstances like this before; I had grown up with absolutely everything I ever wanted. I attended private schools back in Colombia. We had a live-in maid. Life was perfect.

I now realize that if you grow up in poverty, you develop the ability to cope because you don't know any better. You've never been in abundance. But if you go from having wealth to having nothing, it's very difficult because of the dramatic change in lifestyle. However, the one constant source of joy in my life during that time was playing soccer.

One day after a soccer tournament, a gentleman came over to me and complimented my performance. He asked me if I wanted to play soccer in Europe. I had no other opportunities to pursue. The chance to play soccer for a living and to travel the world was a dream come true. I immediately said yes.

I was sent on a flight over to Zaragoza, Spain, and was told I would be participating in a tryout for a team there called Real Zaragoza. A few days later, I went to Ciudad Deportiva—which means the sports city—for a tryout. I distinctly remember sitting in the changing room putting on my cleats. Then I walked out on to the field. I did really well that day.

I think I blew the minds of the recruits, because I am a little guy who is about 5-foot-6 or 5-foot-7. I probably weighed about one hundred and thirty-five pounds at the time. I easily dribbled around defenders and made a good impression. I was asked to join the team and immediately agreed.

I soon found myself traveling with the team to different exotic locations, meeting new people and, best of all—getting paid to play the game I loved. Shortly after that—about three years later—I ended up playing for a team called Tecos in Guadalajara, Mexico. It was a fantastic experience, and I was having the time of my life.

Everything was going great until, at the age of 24, my career as a professional athlete came to a halt with an injury. I found myself sitting on the bench, watching the action from the sidelines. I started to reconsider my life and think about what I wanted to do with myself.

My aunt lived in Tampa, Florida. I reached out to her about staying with her. She said I could, and I decided to come back to the United States. I started going to school. I got a part-time job at Citibank.

It was a very different life from being a soccer player, and I became depressed. I expected to have a full soccer career and retire when I was in my 30's, not at the age of 24. I knew I had to reinvent myself. For about nine months, my depression worsened, as I had no idea what I was going to do with myself.

Every day I would see a guy pass by my condo with a big book under his arm. One day I noticed him and said, "What are you reading?" He replied, "Oh you're going to love this book. It's going to change your life forever. You can borrow it for seven days, but I want it back in seven days." I held this thick, 400-page book in my hands called *Awaken the Giant Within,* by Tony Robbins. I read the entire book in only four days. It gave me the inspiration and the motivation that I needed to get out of that bad place.

I decided that I was going to be better off than I was when I was playing soccer. And I was going to prove to people that I could get back on my feet and be successful. I decided to get into the fitness industry because that was my first love.

I always admired the athletic trainers and personal trainers that worked with me while I played soccer. So, I acquired the necessary certifications and launched my first business: a 400-square foot gym. Everyone told me not to do it, and that I was not going to make it; but I had made up my mind.

The next three years the business was very successful. I was getting there at 6:00 in the morning and then leaving at around 10:00 at night. So, there were long days, but the business was doing well financially. I was just interested in making money and saving money and becoming something. As a result, I fully immersed myself in the world of personal development.

My mantra was that if I had enough money, and I had enough time, I could figure things out. So, God was pushed to the sidelines. I felt like I was making all these things happen through my willpower and my grit. Why do I need God when I was already accomplishing so much on my own? I became an atheist or humanist. I believed I was capable of doing everything without God.

From the age of 24 to about 33, I was lost in the world of personal development. I achieved a lot and found myself chasing shiny objects. I had a steady girlfriend, but I had many other girlfriends on the side.

The truth is, I was a complete mess. I was drinking heavily on the weekends and living a very incongruent life. On Monday through Friday I was preaching health and wellness, yet on the weekends I was destroying my body. I did that until the age of 33, when everything came crashing down. The girl I dated for five years decided to leave me. I woke up one morning and noticed that it felt like my heart was skipping a beat. I went to the doctor's office and was given an EKG to find out more.

The doctor told me I had an atrial fibrillation in my heart, and I could never drink again. If I did, I could have a stroke.

At first, I felt like this was exactly what I needed in my life. This meant I could never drink again and move on to a new life. However, two weeks later, my drinking was worse. I started drinking myself into the grave. One Sunday morning, I was depressed and started writing a suicide note to my sister.

At that moment, I realized that I was in a really bad place, and I decided to reach out to someone I knew in my building.

He was my age and had a very positive demeanor. I would often bump into him when I was on my way home from the club. He would be on his way back from church with a Bible under his arm. I would regularly chat with him and tell him to put down the Bible and to go party with me. He would always laugh and tell me that he had left that life behind and invite me to church. I would shrug it off and tell him that church was not for me.

So that morning when I had reached my all-time low point, he crossed my mind. I decided to give him a call. I told him that I didn't think I had another two days in me. He immediately came to my room and sat across from me. He said, "Let me tell you what God's doing in my life." Once he said that I said, "You're going to have to give me something else, because I don't believe in God."

And he stood up really straight. He said, "Well, God is all I have for you." And I said, "Okay, I don't know what that means."
He said, "Well, what are you doing tonight?" And I said, "Well, I was going to kill myself, but if you have better plans, let's go do that." He chuckled a little, and we got in his car to go to church.

I had some preconceived notions of what church was like from growing up in the Catholic Church. When I walked into this building, I saw it was modern. I saw two things I love: coffee and pretty women. I thought to myself, if this is Jesus, I am in! I walked into the sanctuary and was blown away by how beautiful it was. There was a worship team that looked more like an orchestra. I took a seat there in the sanctuary, and the pastor came out in normal clothes and talked about his family. I related to him.

The pastor taught about the book of Job. The book of Job is about the guy that was faithful to God. Job had anything and everything a man would ever want. God put Job through a time of testing; and during that time, Job lost absolutely everything. He got sick, his kids died, and all these bad things happened. I resonated so much with that story. I thought it was a great story.

When the service was over, I looked at my buddy and said, "Ok that was great, let's go." He replied, "No, let's go to the prayer team."

So, we went over to the prayer team. And this young guy came up to me and asked me what we were praying for. I told him, "Are you ready for this?" He said, "Sure." I said, "Look, I've been doing drugs for two days, and I've been drinking alcohol. I don't believe in God. I have no idea why I'm here, and I'm feeling really awkward now talking about all of my dirty laundry to a stranger." He just looked at me and said, "Okay. Close your eyes, and we'll pray."

He started praying for me and that moment thoughts started flooding in my mind. What am I doing here? This is awkward. I started sweating. Much heavier than normal. At this point, I was sweating like I do when I'm at the gym. I just kept thinking I was sweating because I was nervous and that praying over me was awkward.

At that moment, I started to feel like I had put my finger in an electrical socket. Electricity flowed through my body, and I started bawling like a baby. I didn't even know why I was crying. Most people asked me if I was sad and my response to that is that I wasn't sad.

I had believed happiness comes through achievements, and I had had plenty of those. Instead, for the very first time in my life, I felt joy. And I felt this joy that had nothing to do with my external circumstances. Obviously, I was going through a very tough time, but I felt this relief like a 200-pound weight had been removed from my shoulders.

I walked out of that church that day, and my life radically changed for the better. I became a Christian a couple of months later. I got baptized. I stopped chasing women. I stopped drinking alcohol, and I started devouring the scriptures trying to understand the Bible.

It's been seven years since I completely reshaped my life. Shortly after I became a Christian, I decided to sell my business.

I had a gym that was doing really well with trainers and all the equipment a fitness facility would ever want. I sold it to a guy for twenty-five thousand dollars. He had just moved to Florida from California. I gave him everything and walked away from it. I wanted to go straight into ministry. I didn't want to go to seminary or take time to prepare for such changes in my life.

I thought this was just like a business, so I just dropped everything. I was eager to get into the ministry. Thankfully, God stopped this. For two years I experienced what I call my "desert time." It was a time where God was stripping away anything that I had used as a crutch. Things such as money and influence—the original goals I had for my business. I voluntarily let go of everything and spent my time devouring scripture, praying, fasting, and asking God for His will. I found myself depending strictly on God during that time. I asked God what he wanted me to do next, and in my heart, God spoke to me.

He said that I had a ministry. And so, in a very argumentative way, I said, "Okay, God. That's great. But I don't have the money to start this again. So, I don't know what we're going to do." Once again in my heart, God said, "I will provide."

Shortly after that, some new people started coming into my life. I met this incredible woman named Ana. Four months after we met, we got married. I had an incredible experience dating my wife. In the past, I had never dated and kept it holy.

God carried me incredibly well through that whole situation. In prayer, God said that he wanted me to use my fitness ministry to be a lighthouse for him. I had no idea how we were going to do that.

Philippians 4:13 (ESV) says, "I can do all things through him who strengthens me." We launched our business with the name Fit Method 413. Today we have an ongoing joke where I say we lead more people doing squats and lunges to the Lord than most churches do on any Sunday. It's been an incredible platform for evangelism.

Chapter 2
Preparing Mind, Body and Spirit

We know for a fact that humans have three parts. These are the mind, body and spirit. The Bible says the spirit (or soul) encompasses the mind, will, and emotions.

The Mind
Aspects of the Mind

The mind plays an important role in your body. I'm sure you've heard the saying that "attitude is everything." While I don't fully agree with this, I do think that the thoughts we think and the attitude we have act as lenses through which our life is viewed. In Romans 12:2 (ESV) the apostle Paul said, "Do not conform any longer to the patterns of this world but be transformed by the renewing of your mind. Then you will be able to test and prove what God's will is—his good, pleasing, and perfect will."

In this passage, the apostle Paul is encouraging believers to renew their mind through the Word of God. I find it interesting that he first spoke about the mind. In a lot of religious circles, we tend to see people neglect the mind; but here in this passage, the apostle Paul talks about the mind first. The mind is a very important part of our life: everything we do starts as a thought. This is how the cognitive process works. We think, we feel, and we act.

When you work out, you develop more mental toughness. You build grit. Why? When you endure pain for forty-five minutes to an hour (or however long your workout is), you are really pushing your mind to be subject to pain.
When you endure pain and being uncomfortable, your mind gets tougher.

I love this saying you've probably heard before: "How you do anything is how you do everything." So when you go through painful experiences—even when working out—then you can translate those disciplines into other areas of your life. Those grueling workouts that make you want to vomit actually strengthen the mind.

First you feel the tension in your muscles, and the next couple of days you feel sore. At the same time, you know your body is getting stronger. All of these things allow your mind to get stronger. On top of that, the mental acuity that comes from working out allows the mind to reach new levels of focus. You'll find yourself thinking more clearly and more creatively.

All these things come from embracing fitness. There's also another part to working out and the mind: you can become more confident. I'm not talking about being prideful or arrogant. Rather, I'm simply talking about knowing that you have the ability to endure these challenges.

When you volunteer to face the adversity of working out, a feeling of certainty starts to grow inside of you. You know that you can handle pain and that you can do difficult things.

As you continue to show up, you will rise to the challenge and do things you didn't think you could do. Best of all, your confidence will start to build.

When you find yourself going through other tough situations in life, your subconscious mind automatically kicks in and reminds you that you've already faced difficult challenges before. You'll know that you can make it through this situation, just like you went through that workout.

In many sports—such as golf, tennis, and bodybuilding—athletes that go through intense workouts develop higher levels of mental focus. I'm a perfect example of that. As a child, I had a learning disability. I was unable to concentrate. I couldn't read a book. It turns out I had dyslexia. I started exercising at a very young age. I enrolled in martial arts from ages five to nine, and then I picked up soccer.

As I continued to participate in sports, my ability to focus developed. I became more structured, and my levels of concentration improved as well. There are endless possibilities once you embrace fitness and participate in activities that strengthen your mind.

Aspects of the Will

Let's move on to the area of will. The will is basically the ability to move forward and do things. In other words, we may also call this discipline. Fitness is an incredible way to embrace discipline. Once again, I think it is worth revisiting this saying: "How you do anything is how you do everything." I strongly believe that.

When you can build up your levels of discipline in something hard like fitness, that pain can carry forward into other areas. For example, you can become very disciplined in your devotional time, in your schoolwork or in anything that you embrace in life.

Fitness and discipline are clearly linked together. Both bring consistency and structure into your life. Discipline is also the perfect antidote for laziness. If you struggle in this area, it could be a matter of temperament.

There is one temperament called the Phlegmatic. The Phlegmatic tends to be a little slower and a little harder to motivate. I have always said that the antidote for the Phlegmatic is having an exercise routine and establishing new habits.

J.T. Tapias

Getting into those habits of working out can really push someone out of their comfort zone. This simple adjustment into your schedule will change everything for you.

In addition, the will—in combination with fitness—can cure substance abuse. You know my story. I had a substance abuse problem in my life, and I truly believe that the Lord liberated me from that. Through God's help—He strengthened my will. Fitness was an important component of my life. I relied on the Lord, and those workouts helped to treat my anxiety.

Fitness was an amazing way for me to release this tension in my life. When I was stressed throughout the week or had a lot of things going on, I would get a good workout. This physical activity helped me in my recovery process, and praise to God that I have been sober now for more than five years.

Once again, I believe that the Lord did that for me. But fitness was an incredible tool that helped me to heal and recover.

Aspects of the Emotions

Finally, I'd like to talk about emotions. For most of us, our emotions can go up and down and look a lot like going on a rollercoaster. Of course, the Lord will bring peace into your life. That is where peace stems from.

Working out can also help people who suffer from depression. Fitness is an incredible way to get rid of depression through the release of chemicals that allow us to be happy. These happy chemicals, such as dopamine, epinephrine, and serotonin, are released into the brain through physical training; and they help in that process of overcoming depression.

If you're depressed or have thoughts of negativity in your life, fitness can impact your emotions in a positive way. When you participate in a hard workout such as going for a run or lifting weights for 45 minutes to an hour, the physical activity can help you move past feelings of depression or anxiety.

The same thing goes for stress. I believe that in many cases stress is just energy that is bottled up and hasn't been channeled in a proper way. Fitness is an excellent strategy to release stress in a healthy way and to channel that energy in a positive way.

In my counseling practice, I meet many people experiencing feelings of anxiety (fear) and exile. One of the main things that we talk about is incorporating a fitness routine into their lives and changing their eating habits.

When we are not eating properly—when we're not moving—we are filled with toxins. These toxins are not only in our body, they're also in our mind. They affect our emotional realm, so that's one of the first things that I talk to people about when they're experiencing this roller coaster of emotions. The way to stabilize these feelings is with proper nutrition, exercise, counseling, and the Word of God.

These three areas—the mind, the will, and emotions—impact our cognitive process. We think, we feel, and we act. Fitness impacts all these areas in positive ways.

If you're facing any challenging mental situations, I would highly encourage you to embrace a fitness routine to strengthen your mind. It's going to impact your will. It's going to impact your emotions, and you're going to be in a great place.

The Spirit

I find that fitness is an incredible way to embrace the Spirit of God. There is a close connection between physical fitness and the Spirit of God.

1 Corinthians 6:19-20 (ESV) says, "Or do you not know that your body is a temple of the Holy Spirit within you, whom you have from God? You are not your own, for you were bought with a price. So glorify God in your body."

This scripture clearly states that as Christians the Holy Spirit dwells in us. Our body is what we're showing the world. And so, don't we want to show the world the best face of Christianity? Now don't get me wrong: this is not a vain statement that "You have to look a certain way." No, this is simply talking about congruency in our Christian walk.

It is said that within the first five to seven seconds people know if we are not taking care of our body. It's evident by the way we look. Other people know if we are carrying an extra fifteen, twenty, twenty-five, or fifty pounds. This communicates that there is an area of our lives that we are not taking care of that needs attention.

Since we want to have a great testimony in the eyes of the world, these things are very important for the believer.

If you are a non-believer, there is also something for you. I truly believe that fitness is an incredible vehicle to connect to God.

When most people develop a fitness routine and start going to a gym, they don't necessarily come in with the idea that they're going to get into a relationship with God or that they're going to embrace Jesus. They come through the doors with other objectives: they want to get six-pack abs or to get larger biceps.

After someone participates in a tough workout, the body starts to release toxins. This is the process that we go through when we sweat. When we endure pain through our workouts, we are releasing lactic acid in our muscles and we're getting rid of toxins. If you look at the word toxin, it is defined as a poison. It's a poison that's inside of our body: very much like sin.

A lot of times people consider only the literal form of toxins: the ones that come from food and the environment. But what about the toxins inside us due to sin? I truly believe that through exercise you can develop a higher level of sensitivity to God's voice.

If you ever watch an interview with an athlete, oftentimes these individuals are giving thanks to God. It's something that you'll hear ninety-nine percent of the time when they interview an athlete. Now, saying this doesn't mean that they're necessarily godly people; I just find it interesting that athletes are often attuned to the things of God.

I truly believe that it has a lot to do with releasing toxins and becoming sensitive to the voice of God. And when we release all these toxins from our body, we have mental clarity.

When you participate in exercise, your body releases endorphins, and you have mental clarity. This clarity allows us to embrace God and be more sensitive to the voice of God. If you happen to be in the presence of a good evangelist who is bold about his or her faith and you've been exercising for at least 30 days, you're going to be more receptive to the things of God.

As incredible as this may seem, I've experienced this now for fifteen years in operating four gyms. I've seen countless people transform their lives in many ways. While Fit Method 4:13 is based on a platform of fitness, it is also a platform for relational discipleship. I often see people coming to Christ through physical fitness. I often say that Fit Method 4:13 leads more people to the Lord doing squats and lunges than most churches do on any Sunday. And I believe this component is so important.

Once people get active and start moving, they start eating properly. They start feeling better, and, in that process of doing that, they also develop sensitivity to the voice of God. Many times, embracing exercise is also a way to embrace the Spirit.

Part of the reason for this is because when you exercise, you develop discipline. We live in a very undisciplined world, so when you build up self-discipline, it has the power to change your life. Every believer needs discipline to study scripture. You need discipline for prayer. You also need discipline for fasting.

These are the spiritual disciplines that a believer needs to have in his life in order to thrive, in order to be in victory.

When you participate in physical exercise, doing something physical is often translated into a spiritual realm. This is a great example of the connection between the physical body and the spirit working hand in hand. I believe that discipline enables a believer to say "no" to temptation. And this is such an important thing for the believer.

There are many temptations in the world, but as believers, we are called to live a different kind of life. We are called to live counterculture to the world, so often we have to say "no" to many things and to deny our flesh.

In 1 Corinthians, the apostle Paul talks about this clearly. 1 Corinthians 9:25-27 (ESV) says, "Every athlete exercises self-control in all things. They do it to receive a perishable wreath, but we an imperishable. So I do not run aimlessly; I do not box as one beating the air. But I discipline my body and keep it under control, lest after preaching to others I myself should be disqualified."

In these verses, the apostle Paul is speaking about salvation and about being congruent. These are the reasons why he beats his body, why he disciplines his body. I'm pretty sure the apostle Paul wasn't doing burpees and bench presses.

However, he was disciplining himself and saying no to the world and killing the flesh. Fitness is an incredible way to create this form of discipline when you are consistent with your workouts. When the temptations of the world come your way, it becomes easier for you to resist. That is why I say that fitness is such an incredible vehicle to embrace the spirit. Here's another example: 1 Corinthians 6:19 (ESV) says, "Do you not know that your body is a temple of the Holy Spirit within you, whom you have from God? You are not your own."

We should embrace proper eating and incorporate physical fitness into our lives to be strong and to have the energy needed for ministry. This allows us to exemplify congruency in our walk and all the things we do.

The Body

I know most people see me as a fitness and nutrition coach, so it would be easy to assume that I would address the body before addressing anything else. I addressed the mind first, spirit second, and the body is actually last. I did this because we are often overwhelmed with fitness and nutrition information. I left this section last because I wanted to give you a break. I'm going to share a couple facts with you—but only a handful that matter to help you understand the problem at hand. The U.S. is the most obese country in the world. More than 1 in 3 adults is considered overweight. More than 2 in 3 adults are said to be overweight or obese.

These classifications are based on body mass index or BMI. This is an individual's weight divided by his height and is often related to the amount of fat in the body. When an adult has a BMI of 25-29.9 percent, he is considered overweight; 30 percent to 39.9 percent is considered obese; 40 percent or higher is extreme obesity. [1]

Obesity is a significant risk factor for cardiovascular disease, which is one of the leading causes of death here in the United States. Inactivity and poor eating habits basically kill 670,000 people a year. A little over a million people a year are dying because of inactivity and bad eating habits. [2]

Okay, that's it for the facts. It is clear we have a problem here in the United States. However, I think there could be a larger problem at hand. The Bible says the Devil's agenda is to steal, kill and destroy. So, the question must be asked: could the Devil have his hand in this? I think the answer to this is very clear.

In the previous section, I mentioned that toxins are defined as poisons. We generally think of toxins as literal poisons that are in our body. I also correlated toxins with sin. Sin is a toxin in our mind that affects all areas of life. As believers, when we start to cleanse our body, we're also cleansing that sin toxin that is inside of us. Whether it comes through gluttony or poor self-control, I believe that sin is connected to the many challenges people have with their health.

Many people are 15 to 25 pounds overweight. Often this can be attributed to eating at fast food restaurants but being overweight is not necessarily because of fast food. Fast food is all over the world, yet individuals in the United States are the most obese. I think that here in America obesity really stems from busy lifestyles. People are chasing the American dream. People are living above their means and being completely stressed out and being emotional eaters.

As a counselor with a master's degree in substance abuse and eating disorders, when I talk to counselees about this situation, I regularly see that many people have a bad relationship with food.

What do I mean by a bad relationship with food? A bad relationship with food is when people turn to food for emotional reasons. In other words, when some people have a bad day or feel a void inside, food is the automatic response to the situation. Food becomes a crutch just like alcohol or other drugs. These poor choices have the potential to cause great harm to our bodies and can even lead to premature death. Therefore, it is very clear that we need to be knowledgeable about our health choices.

However, I have never heard a pastor or any spiritual leader really talk about the subject of nutrition or even the subject of gluttony in the church. We know all the obvious sins: don't murder, don't covet, don't commit adultery and all of the things often mentioned in church. We never hear pastors talking about gluttony or nutrition.

Gluttony is really based in the area of self-control. As a believer, if you don't have self-control, then you're not going to have a victorious life in Christ. You can love the Lord. You can be saved and when you die, you'll go into his presence. But in this world, you're going to suffer if you have no self-control.

The body has been neglected for many years in the church. I believe it's time for this new generation of believers to embrace the body—not from a vain perspective—in a way that honors God. I Corinthians 6:19 tells us that we are a temple of the Holy Spirit, that our bodies are to represent our testimony through congruency.

This topic is one of the things that I am highly passionate about. I want to bring this message to the church.

Outside of the church, we use that as a platform for evangelism, so there are many incredible ways to use this topic for both believers and non-believers. If you're a believer and you're struggling with being overweight, I challenge you to add in the components of proper nutrition and movement as a way to glorify God.

If someone ignores this important area in his life, he is actually sinning against God through lack of self-control. He is probably engaging in gluttony, and all these sins are the same in the eyes of God. The Bible is not a big book with separate rules; they all work in harmony. If someone is guilty of one form of sin, he is also guilty of the other. While the sin may not be murder, if someone is being a glutton and has no self-control, he is just like a murderer in that he has committed a sin.

I want to bring that awareness to believers, to help the believer understand that being physically fit is not about vanity. Rather, it is a way to embrace God. It's a way to show congruency in his walk. We are always looking to project and embrace our testimony, so this is a fantastic way to do it.

I hope that you heed my advice and move forward to show the world that when we live in Christ, we live in victory in all areas—even in the physical realm.

When you truly understand these three areas—the mind, spirit, and body--it becomes clear that physical fitness is a way to serve God and connect with Him. Instead of viewing physical health as something completely separate from spiritual and mental health, it's obvious that it truly plays a critical role in both areas.

Chapter 3
Understanding Human Temperament Types

There are five kinds of temperaments and each one has unique strengths and challenges regarding the Empty Your Bucket Plan. Whenever a participant begins the Empty Your Bucket Plan, I have the individual take a temperament test that allows me to customize a plan that meets his needs. Knowledge of temperament allows me to be sensitive to each participant's strengths as well as his or her weaknesses.

The following pages include a breakdown of the five temperament types: Choleric, Sanguine, Supine, Phlegmatic, and Melancholic. Each temperament has its own unique strengths and weaknesses, but all are created to bring glory to God. I find it a pleasure to work with each one to pursue healthy living.

Here is a simple test that you can take on your own to help identify which temperament you are. Please keep in mind that this does not replace the official temperament assessment. If you would like to take the official assessment, please email me at emptyyourbucket@gmail.com, and I will follow up with you.

For this sample assessment, go through each temperament trait and rate yourself on a scale from 1 to 5, with 1 being not at all me and 5 being definitely me. Add up your totals. Whichever total score is the highest is likely your temperament type. Where do you find yourself on this scale? That is likely your temperament.

TEMPERAMENTS

CHOLERIC					
	1	2	3	4	5
Optimistic					
Task Oriented					
Confident					
Self Sufficient					
Activist					
Dominant					
Passionate					
Leader					
Constant					
Willful					
Easily provoked					
Insensitive					
Little Sympathy					
Determined					
Decision oriented					
Sarcastic					
Practical					
Direct					

SANGUINE	1	2	3	4	5
Emotional					
Compassionate					
Impractical					
Easily discouraged					
Undisciplined					
Uncommitted					
Weak Will					
Talkative					
Charming					
Friendly					
Agitated					
Low concentration					
Present Focused					
Egotistical					
Impulsive					
Unpunctual					
Optimistic					
Open					

SUPINE	1	2	3	4	5
Giving					
Serve others					
Demanding					
Relationship oriented					
Fear of rejection					
Dependent					
Not expressive					
Victim					
Inability to initiate love					
Difficulty saying no					
Weak willed					
Harboring Anger					
Introverted & Extroverted					
Gentle Spirit					
Hurt Feelings					
Manipulative					
Defensive					
Needs recognition					

PHLEGMATIC

	1	2	3	4	5
Quiet					
Pessimistic					
Introvert					
Gentle					
Observant					
Doubtful					
Slow paced					
Easy going					
Calm					
Efficient					
Trustworthy					
Dry Humored					
Joker					
Selfish					
Organized					
Frugal					
Stubborn					
Efficient under pressure					

MELANCHOLIC

	1	2	3	4	5
Deep emotions					
Sensitive					
Egocentric					
Easily Offended					
Selfless					
Loyal friend					
Low profile					
Suspicious					
Introspective					
Perfectionist					
Rancorous					
Creative					
Moody					
Critical					
Doubtful					
Pessimistic					
Idealistic					
Introvert					

Choleric Summary

The Choleric can be viewed as a developer. He may be seen in construction supervision, coaching or law enforcement. Many entrepreneurs are Choleric. A Choleric is extremely goal- or task-oriented in leading others. In most situations, this temperament will do whatever it takes to achieve a goal.

Having a mentor is often very helpful for Cholerics because it forces them to be humble and listen. If you're hiring a mentor or coach and you don't listen to them, you are not learning or growing from the experience. Even if the mentor is wrong, a lesson in humility helps make you grow in wisdom.

In this day and age, it is important to find win-win situations more than it is to win by yourself. Cholerics can find great strength in being quiet and empowering others to lead. When you listen to others, it leads to reflection about where you can grow as a leader.

It is also important for a Choleric to embrace a positive path by listening to others and taking the backseat instead of always trying to be in control.

Even if a Choleric achieves his goals or wins over the competition, if he burns bridges and hurts people, the ends do not justify the means. That's why it is essential for this temperament to reframe their approach and be the best version of themselves.

Choleric Strengths

Cholerics are natural leaders as they are normally bold, strong-willed, and don't sugar coat things. When I was a kid in third grade through sixth grade, I wasn't voted to be the soccer team captain—I just took on the role naturally.

It is important to use a Choleric's determination as an advantage when implementing the Empty Your Bucket Plan. Cholerics are not easily discouraged; they are independent and self-sufficient. Knowing that this type often has a compulsive need for change, mix up his workout routine. Allow him to choose the order of his workout: he may want to roll some dice or spin a wheel.

This type is also very goal driven, so focus on the goal at hand. Emphasize the goal as it will help the individual focus on the task at hand so he can accomplish it. It is important not to try to control a Choleric. Rather, give them recognition for accomplishments. Give them opportunities to take on tasks and responsibilities.

Choleric Challenges

Cholerics face some unique challenges. This temperament tends to be overbearing, or dominant. Cholerics tend to burn bridges and often come across as not being sensitive. While a Choleric doesn't intend on burning bridges, he feels the need to fix things right now. This mindset does not come from a bad place—it comes from a place of wanting to help. Cholerics are often fueled by anger or competition. Anger is a catabolic emotion that breaks down the body, so it is not a positive emotion to fuel motivation. Perhaps something negative happened in the past. In some cases, Cholerics are fueled by competition, the need for importance, the need to shine or wanting the spotlight.

These traits or approaches can be dangerous if someone is not aware of his or her temperament. For example, many Cholerics have the need to have the last word. This can be destructive because you learn more when you are quiet.

In some extreme cases, Cholerics may be hot-tempered and use people. Although everyone uses people to some degree, the Choleric temperament may think of themselves as people motivators and use people on a regular basis. They become easily frustrated in their attempts to "motivate" people. They harbor anger and can be cruel and abusive.

How Cholerics Interact with Others

Cholerics need time alone. Do not force them to socialize. They are independent. Do not try to control them or tell them what to do. They need recognition for their accomplishments. Give them opportunities to achieve those accomplishments. Cholerics are task-oriented and can be great leaders. It is helpful to give them opportunities to take on responsibilities and make decisions.

Sanguine Summary

A sanguine believes life is an exciting and fun-filled experience. This temperament is very social, charismatic and liked by others. Many Sanguines are also enthusiastic, warm and optimistic. A sanguine sees the bright side of life as well as the good in other people. They genuinely like people. As a result, they are rarely found alone, and freely interact with people.

Sanguines are talkative; always the life of the party; apt to take on behavior and morals of the people around them; and have a lot of energy.

Some Sanguines are impulsive, undisciplined, rude, prone to exaggerate, and have the need to appear successful (even to the point of exaggeration). In some cases, a Sanguine will ignore responsibilities in order to be with people.

Sanguine Strengths

It is highly recommended that this temperament work with an accountability partner or coach. The Sanguine should log all their meals, cardio, and tasks and then share their results. This allows them to stay more engaged.

Sanguines enjoy circuit training because it keeps them moving and compliments their high energy. The kind of music that is played can help make working out an event. Changing environments can also keep Sanguines engaged. A couple of lower-cost gym memberships can give this temperament a needed change of pace to boost interaction.

Sanguine Challenges

Anytime this temperament is isolated from people, they feel stressed and may even become depressed. However, when people are around them and they are the center of attention, they feel energized. Typically, they sustain their energy levels well. For the most part, a Sanguine either has high energy or no energy. When Sanguines are challenged and not bored, their energy levels soar. To avoid boredom, changing up routine, environment and even music can boost a Sanguine's energy levels.

Food preparation is a common struggle for Sanguines because it is normally something done alone. Sanguines struggle with being alone or getting bored, so the key is to make food prep an event. You could invite friends over for dinner and then do the food prep together or even just join others at their home when they do food prep.

Even going to the grocery store together and then doing food prep after you buy the groceries could increase accountability and engagement.

The sanguine temperament needs to commit all their plans to the Lord and ask for God to fill them with the consistency, discipline and clarity that they need to be successful.

How Sanguines Interact with Others

Sanguines hate to be alone, need to be center stage, want to be popular, and thrive on compliments. Sanguines benefit greatly from having an accountability coach or partner for a designated amount of time (such as 90 days).

Supine Summary

A Supine is dependable and intensely loyal. They have a great capacity for service, like people and have a sincere desire to serve others. When young, this temperament is often tormented and abused by other children. They are typically slow to fight back. Instead, they often internalize their anger. They may even believe they deserve the treatment they receive. As a result, males may struggle with suppressing anger over time, harboring anger as "hurt feelings."

A Supine is always inclined to seek out others' advice when trying to make decisions. Supines often feel inadequate and consider themselves incapable of making good decisions on their own. They may seek out the counsel of several people and become quite confused if they receive differing opinions.

Supine Strengths

Once a level of loyalty is established, a Supine can be a fantastic client who accomplishes great results. Find a common bonding point to build up loyalty and trust. It doesn't have to be serious: a bonding point could start out with sports, a movie or music. Then reveal more of yourself to the Supine. Show you are dependable by being prompt with your time. Set a schedule for the Supine to show how dependable they are. Encourage the client. With their great capacity to respond to love, this is very important.

Supine Challenges

A Supine may expect others to read their mind and know what they want. They also have a high fear of rejection. Oftentimes, a Supine will not make decisions on their own or execute on their ideas.

Supines experience hurt feelings if someone makes a decision for them without their input. When they feel hurt in this way, it angers them.

Supines have a weak will when they are internally driven. They need to be directed in a unique way that motivates them. They need guidance and direction by someone who will hold their hand and reward them with words and affirm them. This temperament responds positively to compliments and edification that lifts them up.

How Supines Interact with Others

The Supine temperament needs constant reassurance and avoids making decisions (or makes decisions cautiously). They need social relationships and like people.

Supines need to find a trainer that they respect. The trainer needs to be a teacher who truly cares and is also passionate about the individual's goals.

A great question for a Supine to ask is, "Why did you become a trainer?" A supine wants to hear, "I'm motivated to help others achieve their goals."

Often a Supine will say, "I've worked out all my life, and I've never seen any results." The coach needs to be someone who says, "I know, I understand. But, trust me, this time will be different." Proper coaching can give the individual the confidence they need to succeed.

The trainer needs to be loving and supportive in their interactions. If the Supine feels the trainer is truly interested in their success, they will follow the directions very closely.

Being able to take the lessons and translate them into day-to-day life is essential for a Supine's success. One great way to do this is to write down the directions clearly. Don't give general guidelines to a Supine; rather, give them a list of instructions. Then follow up with them promptly. Supines have a need for accountability.

Phlegmatic Summary

A Phlegmatic person is able to perform tedious tasks, relates to both tasks and people, and is easy going. Overall, Phlegmatics are extremely efficient and perfectionistic. The Phlegmatic can function quite well in a hostile social setting. Nothing "ruffles their feathers." They like calm and steady lives, free of surprises.

Often Phlegmatics are very quiet and do not share their own inner thoughts readily, as they fear judgment and don't wish to bother others by waffling on about themselves.

They are, however, excellent and attentive listeners who will quietly and politely take in and absorb the conversations of their friends. They always pay attention and will offer supportive feedback rather than criticism or advice. They'd never say things like, "I am bored now," as if it's the duty of others to entertain them.

Since they hate to offend or hurt others, they generally don't ever resort to aggressive insults or attacks. Belittling or hurting another makes them feel bad, not "powerful and in control" or amused, so they'll worry about having done this accidentally. They could be described as "nice guys/girls" or, more horribly, "doormats" by those with different temperaments.

Phlegmatics do not often express their emotions. While the Sanguine might whoop and cheer and jump for joy at the slightest provocation, Phlegmatics are unlikely to express more than a smile or a frown. A Phlegmatic's emotions are mostly internalized, so they often rely on others ordering them to do things to get motivation.

Phlegmatic Strengths

For the most part, Phlegmatics have low-key personalities and are easygoing and relaxed.

Some might even describe them as calm, cool, and collected. The Phlegmatic works slowly, but perseveringly, if his work does not require much thinking. In addition, Phlegmatics work well under pressure and are very reliable.

Phlegmatics are not easily exasperated either by offenses, or by failures or sufferings. They remain composed, thoughtful, deliberate, and have a cold, sober, and practical judgment. Phlegmatics have no intense passions and do not demand much of life. In addition, Phlegmatics enjoy good jokes and know how to tell them.

Phlegmatic Challenges

Phlegmatics can be relatively confident in familiar situations—if not necessarily assertive—but panic when placed in new situations. While Phlegmatics do not seek thrills, they often enjoy predictable, quiet, ritualistic lifestyles.

Sometimes this temperament defers to others to make choices and will feel upset or pressured if they must make a decision themselves. This comes from their inability to see themselves in a "leader" role.

They're more likely to travel around than through something; their path is easily changed by others.

How Phlegmatics Interact with Others

Phlegmatics are introverted, so they recharge themselves by spending time alone. They enjoy being with their friends and are very loyal to these friends. They often put others first and will not leave another even if THEY want to, because the other person may not want them to leave.

Melancholy Summary

Melancholies are very creative and intellectual people. They are self-motivated and do not respond to the promise of reward nor the threat of punishment. Some characteristics of a Melancholy include the following: introvert, loner, great thinker, genius-prone, very artistic and creative. Melancholies are often found alone in thought and are perfectionists. They are slow-paced, have a great understanding of tasks and systems, a critical and challenging mind, and see both the pitfalls and the end results of projects.

Melancholies are loyal to their family and friends. If a Melancholy makes a promise, he will keep it. In most cases, if you see a beautiful painting or hear a beautiful piece of music, it was likely created by a Melancholy.

Melancholies are not aggressive and prefer to flee from things that cause them distress. They also love research, and their conclusions must be based on facts.

Melancholies can be efficient and effective leaders. They can create something out of nothing. Be careful not to critique this temperament publicly. Instead, encourage the client and be sensitive to their emotions.

Melancholy Strengths

Melancholies often have a serious view of life. This temperament helps them to find a proper place in the world both in their private life and in their career. They are usually very hard-working, detail-oriented people, who can foresee and consider multiple potential dangers on the horizon.

Melancholies usually possess a sharp and profound intellect. Unwilling to settle for surface knowledge, this temperament delves deeply into a wide range of subjects. They truly want to master the topic at hand. Punishment and rewards have little effect, as Melancholies are often self-motivated. They precisely know their strengths and limitations and rarely take on more than they can do.

Melancholy Challenges

This group tends to procrastinate when working on something that is new or unknown. A Melancholy is often right, so instead of being wrong or failing, a Melancholy will spend extra time in research or do something that is familiar. Sometimes moods will lift them to extreme highs; at other times they will be gloomy and depressed.

A Melancholy may set standards that neither they nor anyone else can meet. However, the Melancholy temperament can become very proficient in new areas if given the time to learn it properly and not be pushed. Encourage them! Work very hard to help them raise their self-esteem by reinforcing the positive and downplaying the negative within the environment.

How Melancholies Interact with Others

This group gets upset—even very angry—when they are wrong. Some Melancholies even have a "my way or the highway" attitude. This outlook typically presents unique challenges when training a Melancholy. For a Melancholy to work well with a coach, he must feel the coach is intellectually superior.

He must respect his coach. A way to build respect could be for the coach to share any certifications, degrees and credentials.

The coach should make sure that the Melancholy keeps logs for food and workouts. The visual aspect of seeing success encourages the Melancholy. This group loves to be praised or complimented. The graphs and charts showing results and achievements will help the individual continue to move forward.

Melancholies are the most introverted of the temperaments in that they crave time alone and are most at ease in their own company.

Accountability calls should be scheduled every seven days. Give specific advice that can be put into action. This will allow the client to paint a picture in his head and move forward. When a coach works with a Melancholy, he needs to be a very clear communicator. Tell the client what you specifically want him to do and why you want him to do it. Then have him document it.

In most cases, a Melancholy makes friends cautiously. He is content to stay in the background and avoids causing attention. Melancholies are critical of others.

Typically, this temperament holds back affection and dislikes those in opposition.

Temperament Theory Conclusions

When temperament theory is applied to the Empty Your Bucket Plan, individuals will find themselves better equipped for success.

Once an individual knows what motivates him best, he will be able to accomplish more. He will be able to be more receptive toward the process of meal planning and consistently working out. If he is having a hard time working out or not getting the desired results, temperament theory can provide valuable insight there as well.

Temperament is different than character or personality. It is God-given, so there is intentionality behind it. The Bible often talks of being yoked--specifically unequally yoked or evenly yoked. The yoke refers to the tool that is put around the neck of an animal such as an ox or donkey. When a yoke fits an animal well, it allows more efficiency with less strain, and requires less energy. This concept also applies to our success as humans. When we are in the right environment, spending time with others who encourage us, and when exercise and nutrition routines match with our temperament, less effort is required.

When you learn more about how you are wired, how to eat, how you can grow with your emotions, mind and spirit, success follows.

Here is an allegory that helps show how this applies to our lives: There was a man who walked into a building and stepped on to the elevator. In a few minutes, the doors opened at the basement of the building and he got out. The man noticed a big table filled with food surrounded by a large group of people. Everyone there seemed upset and ticked off. The man wondered what the problem was, the food looked fantastic.

Then the man noticed that each of the guests at the party had only very large spoons to eat with. The spoons were so big that the guests could not fit the food into their mouths. The guests soon became frustrated and started to argue with each other.

The man went back to the elevator, and the doors opened on the third floor. When he stepped out of the elevator, he saw the same scenario: a dinner party with guests. But this time, everyone was happy. They still had large spoons that were too large to use on their own, but at this party the guests were feeding each other, and everyone was happy.

This is a great allegory for relationships: when someone is not being fed what he needs, he is not going to work efficiently. In addition, he is not going to be motivated to do things such as achieving his goals; he is not going to see eye to eye with his partner.

Once we know our needs and our needs are being met, we are 100 times more efficient.

Chapter 4
The Empty Your Bucket Plan (EYB)

Since I know first-hand how important proper nutrition and physical fitness are in serving Christ, I created a plan to help others get in shape, feel great and look great. I knew the plan would have to be simple and straightforward. No counting macros or calories. No restrictions that would require food to be weighed or to prevent participants from going out to eat.

In my experience, many people see positive results on alternative nutrition plans for the first three to six months; but as time goes on, the weight comes back. Because of this fact, I knew my program would need to provide positive results in thirty to forty days maximum. But, more importantly, I needed to help individuals sustain their results for the rest of their lives. If participants were to ever gain some weight back, that they could easily know how to take it off quickly.

In other words, I needed to create an entire health system from the ground up. If you ask any dietitian, nutritionist, or guru they will tell you that it's impossible. Yet it's happening every day.

It's happening through the art and science that we call Empty Your Bucket Plan.

The Empty Your Bucket Plan is unlike any other diet because it is really simple. As long as you follow a few guidelines, you have the flexibility to eat most foods. One of the main reasons the Empty Your Bucket Plan is easy to implement is because the participant doesn't have to count calories.

A general rule for the Empty Your Bucket Plan is that when you have a meal after 2 PM, it should consist of vegetables and lean proteins, or meal replacement shakes.

Vegetables are very low in macronutrients, and the glycemic surge is very low. As a result, eating vegetables keeps your insulin levels balanced out throughout the day.

The Empty Your Bucket Plan calls for three solid meals and three meal replacement shakes per day. It is quite easy to fit into everyday life.

Not only is the Empty Your Bucket Plan easy to follow, it brings positive results. In my experience, most clients can lose 10 to 12 pounds in one month and also lose 1-2 percent of their body fat. These results are very significant. Once an individual's energy levels increase and he starts looking and feeling better, he will become more motivated. These positive results help individuals stay on track and achieve their goals.

The 80/20 Rule

The 80/20 rule helps you follow the Empty Your Bucket Plan. For 80% of the time, you stick to the plan. The other 20% of the time, you can go off plan. During this off-plan time, you can eat out, eat starchy carbs past 2 PM, have ice cream, chips or whatever you would like to have.

Most diets are restrictive, so they are not sustainable. The first three letters of the word diet say it best: die. Most people feel like they're going to die on a diet. Anything a human being suppresses will eventually come out tenfold.

The Empty Your Bucket Plan allows participants to indulge in the foods they want in a social setting without jeopardizing a healthy, balanced way of life.

From a psychological standpoint it is clear that humans like and need structure to grow. Discipline is a muscle that also needs rest. When you practice the 80/20 rule, it brings that perfect balance of discipline and reward to life.

A Plan for the Whole Family

While some people may be concerned that the Empty Your Bucket Plan may be hard to implement in a family setting, in my experience, the Empty Your Bucket Plan does not affect family dinners in any negative way. If anything, the Empty Your Bucket Plan often encourages the skeptical spouse to get onboard. When a spouse sees their significant other lose a ton of weight, become super energetic and optimistic about life, it becomes very easy to get on board.

The Empty Your Bucket Plan includes recipes that are both delicious and easy to make. One of the key components to the Empty Your Bucket Plan is to keep a steady schedule of eating every three hours and not going more than four hours without eating. This simple step addresses extreme hunger, binge eating, and cravings. On top of that, there will always be food around, which most people love. Here are a few key points to consider:

- You don't exist in a vacuum: you exist in a web of relationships, the most important being your family.
- Being a part of the Empty Your Bucket Plan (and getting healthier) encourages the skeptical family member to join in.

- Take advantage of easy recipes to help your family and spend more time together.
- The steady schedule of eating every 3 hours will reduce binge eating and positively affect your relationships. It will also reduce your irritability and mood swings.

I find that in most cases, actions speak louder than words. When you work out consistently and eat healthy, you demonstrate your commitment and passion for your new lifestyle. Over time, others cannot help but notice, and, in most cases, they will support you and even join in.

The truth is, most people have a constant battle with their inner child. Childhood traumas, insecurities, and past disappointments can become the driving force in life. Often these negative emotions guide us in our adult life, and we are not even aware of it. The challenge comes when we've achieved a desired goal. That negative driving force is no longer useful. Rather, it becomes destructive.

Some people have not decided what they really want to do. They are afraid to get healthy and to lose excess weight. They are in a place of shame and condemnation. For these individuals, I would say that changing your life is not easy, but you can do it. When you take a negative and turn it into something positive, you always move forward. I took all my failures, disappointments, and anger and used those negative experiences as fuel to become the best version of me.

I'm still a work in progress, but anytime I'm stuck in a rut, I remind myself of my past successes and feel better about the future.

3 Concepts to Help You Move Forward

There are three core concepts that can be applied to any area of your life that will work very efficiently. When these concepts are combined with hard work, you will grow.

1) *Clarity* is the ability to know exactly what you want and how you want your goal to come to fruition. Clarity gives you power. For example, when we first get into our cars, we set our GPS. This tool guides us in the direction that we would like to go and always knows the destination. Any plan requires that we have this same kind of GPS in our mind. Clarity comes from this process. I think many people are more motivated by pain than they are by pleasure. Many people start

diets, workout plans, and routines without being mentally ready. It's pivotal to understand why you are doing something. Your "why" needs to be strong enough to carry you through the hard times.

2) *Discipline* Most people cringe when they hear the word discipline. In many cases, the word discipline has a negative connotation.

When we were kids, the word discipline was often interchangeable with the word punishment. As a result, we put up a good fight any time a person, situation, or dynamic introduces any kind of restraint into our lives. While this is true, I have never met a successful person that is not disciplined.

Success requires that we incorporate discipline into our daily routines. One way to look at it is that discipline is a part of our daily habits that guide us in the right direction. Discipline helps us avoid distractions. We need to have Specific, Measurable, Attainable, Reasonable, Time-oriented goals and habits in our lives. These disciplines must be written down and kept no matter what happens or how busy we are. These disciplines allow us to stay organized, efficient, and stress free.

I know this is a challenge. When you start out with the Empty Your Bucket Plan, that is why we incorporate support as a key component in the program. You need help from others to be disciplined at first, and, over time, you become more self-disciplined.

3) *Consistency* is the ability to stay on the right track no matter what comes your way. Our world is filled with distractions that fight for your time, money, energy and attention.

Everyone and everything pull us in a different direction constantly. Family members—even though they often have the best intentions—are notorious for getting us off track.

At the end of my soccer career, I was down to 9 percent body fat and in the best shape of my life. I went home for lunch that day with my mother and she looked at me and said, "Are you okay?" I said, "Yes mom. Why?" She said, "You look so skinny. Are you sure you're not sick?" I realize that my mother was simply worried and wanted to make sure that I was okay. However, if I would've taken her misperception into consideration, I likely would have stopped focusing on fitness, something that has had an incredibly positive effect on my life. Once you've decided what your goal is and start participating in your disciplines rigorously, make sure no one gets you off track.

As you follow these three concepts and stick with them, over time you will see that criticism or negative talk from others will soon turn into praise. Make time to reflect and to connect to your "Why." This simple step can take most people a long way.

I take my coaching clients through an awesome process called "Seven Levels Deep." This process allows the person being coached to reach an emotional "why" for the reason they do what they do. I once heard someone say that emotions are the fast track to the brain. I believe this is very true. This is different from simply being guided by emotions; this process helps us to connect to our deepest desires.

In other words, it is not about a coach or trainer telling someone what to do. Rather, it is important for the participant to connect with *why* they should do it. This will compel and convict the individual to follow through—even in the hardest and most challenging moments. It is pivotal to renew our mind and to establish a new relationship with food (and even our perception of food) in order to succeed with this plan.

The Pillars of EYB

The three main pillars of EYB are:

1) eating every three hours

2) not eating starchy carbs past 2 PM

3) portion control for starches (one to two handfuls for breakfast and or for lunch).

Slow burn cardio and high intensity interval training are also important parts of the Empty Your Bucket Plan, but I'll dive deeper into those later in the book.

While I believe the number of calories you eat and use is important, I'm not an advocate for calorie counting. I know these methods can be successful, but they are not sustainable over the long-term.

Vegetables and protein are low in calories and glycemic index and that is why I recommend a majority of calories come from these foods.

EYB is structured in 30-day increments and should be followed for at least 90 days. Fruit should be avoided during this time for maximum results. The participant has an accountability requirement of one email to their accountability coach per week.

If the person partaking in the program falls off, they should communicate this to the accountability coach, and that coach should establish new ways of engaging the client depending on that person's temperament.

Also, the plan calls for a cheat day or refuel day once every 7 days. This cheat or refuel meal gives the participant an opportunity to keep their mental sanity, and to give the muscle of discipline a break.

Most diets are restrictive and not sustainable. Discipline is a muscle that needs rest. EYB gives you a weekly "release valve." You can still eat most foods within certain guidelines. I believe that anything an individual suppresses will eventually come out tenfold.

The Empty Your Bucket Plan offers individuals both simplicity and structure. Again, here are the basic guidelines of EYB.
- 3 meals and 3 shakes per day
- No fruit for first 90 days
- No carbs after 2 PM

- Vegetables are okay (other than fried onions, carrots, corn and starchy carbohydrates)
- Heart rate monitored cardio. Slow burn or High Intensity Interval Training (HIIT) cardio (please get exact number from your coach). Or you can get that exact number on your own by using these equations:

220 - age x .060 = your low heart rate range.

220 - age x .070 = your high heart rate range.

Chapter 5
The Importance of Sleep

Most people enjoy sleeping. When the alarm clock goes off in the morning, they can't wait until they can go back to bed again. We were all taught from a young age that sleep is important when it comes to our health. As trainers, we agree that sleep is very important when it comes to your health. Yet you might be surprised how and why it affects your fitness results.

Whenever I talk to people about their eating habits, they often tell me that they just don't have enough time. After digging a little further into their lives, we've found that their time crunch all starts in the morning. A lot of people claim they don't have time for the most important meal of the day, breakfast. For most of them, it doesn't even cross their mind that they could get up earlier to ensure they get a good breakfast. Getting up earlier may even sound like a crazy thing to you right now. However, if you truly want to be lean and muscular, you will have to adopt a new attitude.

There are three types of people who try to cut corners at breakfast because they claim to not have enough time.

First, there are the habitual breakfast skippers. Then there are the people who grab whatever is quick but not very healthy on the way out the door. Finally are the people who claim to be eating breakfast, but they don't eat until 2 hours after waking up while they're at work.

If you fit any of these three categories, chances are you will not get 6 meals in each day unless you somehow stack those 2 hours apart, which is brutal and unrealistic.

Let's say you typically sleep for seven hours each night. You go to bed at 11:30 PM and rise at 6:30 AM. In order to have time to prepare and eat your breakfast, you would have to wake up at 6:00 AM.

In your mind, that extra 30 minutes of sleep is something you can't do without. While I understand your need for sleep, I would ask you to look at the big picture. You can still get an extra 30 minutes of sleep if go to bed at 11:00 PM instead of 11:30 PM. If you attempt to eat 6 times a day for a few weeks, you will realize that the amount of sleep you get one day will affect how your eating goes the next day. The days kind of melt together in a sense.

For instance, if you stay up late one evening, you are likely going to get up late the next morning and skimp on breakfast. This one decision will likely throw off your timing with eating meals all day long.

Your other option would be to cut your sleep short to have time for your full breakfast. Only the most dedicated fitness enthusiasts cut back on their sleep. While you might become a dedicated fitness enthusiast at some point in your life, right now you must schedule your sleep to ensure you have enough time to eat breakfast. This meal will give you a good start, which is of the utmost importance, and will help you eat the proper amount of food during each day.

Sleep to Cut Fat

Natural growth hormone plays an important role in the body. Growth hormone helped you grow as a youngster.

Although there is an epidemic of obese children today, you probably remember that you could eat some pretty bad food as a child and still not gain weight. The reason children can eat junk and stay fairly lean is because they are secreting a lot of growth hormone.

However, as you get older, your body produces less growth hormone; and you are not able to eat the things you could as a child and not gain weight.

To be healthy, you want your body to produce the most growth hormone possible. The best way to do this is to get good sleep each night. The human body produces the most growth hormone when it's in REM sleep. In case you don't know what REM sleep is, it's the deepest kind of sleep, when rapid eye movement occurs. It takes a while for your body to reach that level after you've fallen asleep.

You must do whatever you can to ensure a good night's sleep. Make sure your mattress is comfortable. Lower or raise the temperature in your house to a temperature you prefer for sleeping. Keep your room as dark as possible. Put your phone on silent. Do whatever you can to ensure you get a good night's sleep. Your growth hormone levels will rise over time, and your body will support you on your crusade against unwanted fat.

Don't Sleep Your Life or Your Meals Away

Remember, there are only 24 hours in each day. If you sleep for 8 or more hours, you've basically shortened your day to 16 hours or less. This leaves you a shorter amount of time to squeeze in all 6 meals. If you manage to eat breakfast within a few minutes of waking up—which most people don't—you still must get 5 more meals in over the next 14 to 15 hours. Odds are that's not going to happen.

For this reason, I have found that 7 hours of sleep per night is ideal. This much rest should not leave a person feeling tired during the day, and it gives that person an extra hour each day to get all their meals in. People who sleep for 8 hours may be wide awake all day, but they limit their chances of getting all their 6 meals in. People who sleep for 6 hours a night may have plenty of time to eat their 6 meals, but they're always tired.

Being tired can affect other things in your fitness plan such as workouts, going grocery shopping, cooking and other areas. Find the happy medium, and then make a habit of it.

Sleeping seven hours a night spells success when it comes to being lean and muscular. So please be intentional about your sleep. It really makes a difference.

Chapter 6
Nutrition Overview

The ultimate key to successful weight loss is a combination of nutrition, heart rate cardio, and resistance training; but nutrition has the greatest impact.

If you truly want to reach your fitness goals, you must get your nutrition squared away. After training clients for years, I've noticed a big disconnect between how people think they can get fit and how people actually become fit. For example, it seems most people come in thinking they will get in shape purely through exercise. Sadly, that is not the case. There are people who have been exercising for years who have never reached their fitness goals. Nutrition plays a much larger role in a person's fitness level than exercise ever will.

There are also people who have been exercising for six months who have already reached their goals. What's the difference? All parties are putting time, effort and willpower into working out. The difference is that the people who have met their goals have also focused on their nutrition plan.

Consistent, proper nutrition accounts for major factors in the way someone looks and feels. To be successful you must adopt the belief that every single meal on every day, week, month and year counts.

Some people eat healthy occasionally. Truly fit people eat healthy and properly despite plateaus. They do not let issues in life stop them. They pack food to take with them when they go out, order healthy at restaurants, and make good decisions at the grocery store.

The bottom line is that they do not make excuses when it is easy to make an excuse. To find success, it is important to adopt this attitude. In the next few pages, I will focus on important nutritional building blocks.

Complex Carbs

Proper consumption and restriction of complex carbohydrates is vital to overall health.

As your body gets depleted of carbohydrates over extended periods of time, there can be long-term health issues. That is why we recommend depleting carbohydrates for six weeks only. Then you should slowly re-incorporate those complex carbohydrates in your nutrition plan.

Your liver is exposed to extra stress as it manufactures glucose from fats and proteins. As proteins are converted into glycogen, potentially toxic amounts of ammonia are produced. Your body has a more difficult time producing mucus, and the immune system becomes impaired and the risk of pathogenic infections increase. Your body loses the ability to produce compounds called glycoproteins, which are vital to cellular functions.

It is true that many people are essentially cured of their type II diabetes by low carbohydrate diets, but the message is not getting out correctly. People should not succumb to a highly restrictive diet but rather to a lifestyle that allows for an 80/20 process to take place.

Here are a few examples of complex carbs:
Sweet potatoes
Brown rice
Ezekiel bread
Cream of Wheat
Oatmeal
Grits
Whole wheat pasta
Whole wheat bread

Whole wheat wrap
Whole wheat bagel

The carbohydrates listed in bold type on a package signify that the main ingredient in that selection is whole wheat flour. Although whole wheat flour is much better than white flour for fiber and nutrient contents, you should only have one serving of whole wheat flour per day on this program. Choose your whole wheat flour selection wisely. For example, if you would like to have the convenience of a sandwich at lunch, then do not waste your serving by eating toast at breakfast.

Why do complex carbohydrates matter?

Complex carbohydrates play a huge role in the way your body looks. Carbohydrates in general are the preferred energy source for the human body. [3]

In my opinion most Americans are not fat because they eat too much fat. Instead, they are fat because they eat too many carbohydrates. Carbohydrates are typically high in calories per weight than proteins. Calories equate to energy in the body; and when there is more energy in the body than that body will burn, the extra is stored as fat.[4] This is our body's way of surviving famine and long hunts--something less prevalent in modern times.

The body also craves carbohydrates/sugar as quick fuel when hungry. That is why most people would rather have a donut than lettuce. Carbohydrates are also cheaper to make and sell in the U.S., so many people are raised on higher carbohydrate diets and turn to those familiar foods for comfort.

Carbohydrates are not bad, so long as they're consumed in moderation and at the right time of day. Your body needs carbohydrates in the morning if you're looking for quick fuel to start the day. As the day goes on, your body can use the fuel it has stored and keep powering through from meal to snack using what you feed it, if you're feeding yourself protein, carbs, and fats in appropriate amounts.

As we get more tired throughout the day, we may start to crave high sugar and carbohydrate items to keep our body powering. However, this is still an evolutionary trait that we can overcome. We are still powering our bodies using all the fuel we give it throughout the day; the cravings are just stronger as we start to power down. Eating a lot of comfort carbohydrates after work or before bed can often lead to weight gain because we don't need the energy to move and power through our day anymore; thus, the extra calories are stored as fat.

This is comfort eating; and on this program, we're trying to rewire our brains to not trick us into late night carbohydrate-only eating.

Additionally, there is something to be said about the density of the carbohydrates a person eats. The goal is to eat a carbohydrate that is going to digest slowly in your stomach and provide your body with lasting energy. Quick digesting sugars are what lead to insulin spikes in our bodies. An insulin spike sends signals to our brains that there is plenty of food and that prompts our bodies to store excess as fat (in case of famine).[5] You can prevent insulin spikes by eating dense, complex carbohydrates.

A slice of white bread has similar grams of carbohydrates as a slice of whole wheat bread. What makes the whole wheat bread better for you? The answer lies in the density of the wheat. The whole wheat bread is more fibrous because the grain of the wheat is still intact. The fiber is stripped away in white bread, making it easier for your body to digest, causing that insulin spike. This is just one example of how there is more to carbohydrates than the amount a person eats.

Don't be fooled by "healthy" cereal and crackers. Those labels on processed carbohydrate products aren't regulated. For clarity and simplicity, stick to the list of complex carbohydrates on the list for EYB to keep consistency in your diet. Remember, consistency is what will help you reach your long-term weight goals.

Fruits & Vegetables

Some people will tell you to stay away from fruit when losing weight or getting in shape. We say that fruit is absolutely okay but we ask you to stay away from it for the first 90 days. After 90 days it's okay to bring it back into your diet so long as you consume the right kinds of fruit and eat fruit at the right time of day.

Healthy Fruit Consumption

Although all fruit contains fructose, fructose is natural. Fructose will lead to a smaller insulin spike than refined sugar which is found in things like candy. Fruits such as blueberries, strawberries, raspberries, blackberries, kiwis, grapefruit, avocadoes, oranges, cantaloupes, peaches, lemons and limes will not cause much of an insulin spike.

If you choose to veer off this list, you run the risk of severely spiking your insulin with fruits like watermelon. In addition, when you eat fruit is very important. In my opinion, you should never eat fruit after lunch. Even though the fruits I mentioned above have a low amount of sugar, you should not feed your body sugar after lunch time. Not even in small amounts.

Fruit is the only food on earth that can change its nutritional composition with age. Fruit is better for you before completely ripened. For example, a green banana is comprised of 95% good carbohydrates and only 5% sugar. By the time the banana has ripened to the point where it has brown marks on the peel, it is comprised of 95% sugar and only 5% good carbohydrates. The same goes for most fruit on this list.

Fruits always taste sweeter as they ripen because they are converting to simple sugar as they get older. You must do your best to eat fruits that have not fully ripened yet. We've found that apples take the longest time to ripen. If you can only get to the grocery store once a week, we suggest buying a few fruits like pears, bananas or strawberries to eat early in the week. Save your apples for later in the week as they will not be as ripened as your other fruit as the week goes on.

When people eat a diet that is high in fruit or, in other words, fructose, the liver gets overloaded. The fructose in the body starts turning into fat.

Although fruit can be healthy because it's a rich source of clean calories, it can also spike your insulin levels. This is a key driver of many serious diseases today such as obesity, type II diabetes, heart disease and even cancer. For this reason, I highly recommend that clients stay away from fruit in order to allow glycogen storages to be depleted.

After the initial 90-day period in the Empty Your Bucket Plan, I slowly reintroduce carbohydrates and fruit before 2 PM into a participant's diet.
At this point, the body deals well with glycogen and can easily assimilate these nutrients.

How much fruit should you have while maintaining a healthy diet? If the fruit doesn't come in one big piece—like an apple—I recommend you use just one cup of fruit. For instance, you could have one cup of cherries, grapes, blueberries, or strawberries.

Fruit is okay to eat so long as you consume it in moderation and at appropriate times of the day. Although fruit is mostly sugar, the sugar in unaltered fruit is natural and still full of fiber, when compared to juice or other fruit-based items such as fruit snacks. When looking at the glycemic index of fruits, those listed above are considered lower than other fruits because of the added fiber.[6]

Natural sugar will also cause a lower insulin spike than refined sugars, like candy, because of the fiber. [7]

If you choose to buy canned fruits, make sure only to buy those canned in extra light syrup or water. In either case, please avoid drinking the juice, and be sure to rinse the foods before consuming.

The syrup in the cans is just a sugar mixture or maybe fruit juice but is still given added sugar. Typically, fresh fruit is the best choice to ensure there aren't any added sugars or unnecessary calories derailing you from reaching your fitness goals.

Fruits are a great snack to take with you, as they do not need to be cooked or heated. If you know you're going to have to eat at a situation outside of your control (restaurant or other gatherings), a piece of fruit can often be fulfilling and keep us away from tempting chips or fries. You can always pair fruit with a sandwich or a salad for a well-rounded meal.

Are all vegetables the same?

I've seen hundreds of clients over the years coming from all different walks of life, and I realize that there is some confusion when it comes to vegetables. Not all vegetables are helpful when trying to lose weight. Just because a vegetable grows in the ground or on a tree doesn't mean that it is healthy. The vegetables on this list are full of nutrients, vitamins, and minerals that will provide a well-balanced diet.

Stick to this list and you will not have to worry whether you are eating the right vegetables. Do not eat canned vegetables or frozen vegetables with a sauce already cooked together. Both options are high in sodium. When trying to be a health-conscious person, it's best in the long-term to choose fresh or plain frozen vegetables.

Some brands now make low sodium canned varieties of vegetables. If you must use canned vegetables, I suggest choosing one of these to be sure that your daily sodium intake does not increase too much. You should read the ingredients to see if salt is added and avoid those. Salt is naturally in some vegetables and other foods, so it's important to be conscious of your intake.

Fibrous Carbohydrates

Stick with these green and leafy vegetables:

Lettuce
Broccoli
Asparagus
Cauliflower
Spinach
Green beans
Peppers
Mushrooms
Cabbage
Brussels sprouts
Squash
Cucumber
Celery
Artichoke

Avoid these starchy vegetables:

Peas
Carrots
Corn
Fried onions
Squash
Zucchini
Eggplant
Pumpkin
Beets

Why are vegetables important?

The vegetables in the first list above are important for three reasons. First, vegetables contain many vitamins that your body needs to function properly. The second reason is that they are low glycemic index foods that will not allow your blood sugar to drastically spike. [8] The third reason—which is my favorite—is that you can eat large portions of these vegetables without worrying about too many extra calories. Vegetables are the key to feeling full while still working toward weight loss or improving your body. For example, a cup of brussels sprouts only has 38 calories compared to one cup of regular trail mix averaging 693 calories. [9,10]

With this program, when you replace normal snacks with vegetables, you will likely decrease your daily caloric intake. Best of all, you will avoid feeling hungry or deprived.

I recommend that you eat as much of these vegetables as you want, especially later in the day, after 2 PM. Try to stay away from tomatoes, carrots, peas, onions, and corn. Although they are vegetables, they are high on the glycemic index and will cause that unwanted insulin spike in high quantities.

This doesn't mean you can't have them for the rest of your life, just be smart with them. We advise focusing on the green and leafy vegetables above and only adding other vegetables in moderation.

Prepare your vegetables responsibly. For example, a green bean casserole is not a good way to consume vegetables when you are trying to lose weight. For the best weight maintenance, you should not be adding other ingredients to vegetables. Instead, I suggest microwaving, steaming, sautéing, or grilling vegetables. Try to avoid the high sodium seasonings and stick with herbs or light dressings if desired.

Protein

Protein is the building block for muscle. The amino acids which make up protein can be used in the body. These amino acids are essential for muscle growth/maintenance, immunity strength, chemical reactions in the body, and oxygen transfer. Muscle mass is related to creating a lean body because muscle mass can affect your metabolism. Therefore, you cannot obtain a lean body without eating protein.

How much protein should you consume? A person should consume 0.8 grams of protein per kilogram of body weight each day. [11] There is insufficient research to prove a high protein diet can lead to weight loss, but with clients I have seen a difference. When protein is digested it can often keep clients more satiated, which in turn means they feel less deprived on a lower calorie diet. Weight loss maintenance has been shown to be easier with a high protein diet as well. [12]

Protein intake doesn't need to be taken to extreme measures, but I find 15-30 grams of protein at each meal is possible and comfortable for clients. Find what works for you and keep in mind all the benefits of protein.

Here are a few examples of protein values to guide you:

Whole Egg, 1 Large Grade A Egg, raw = 6g protein

Egg White, 1 Egg Equivalent, raw = 3.6g protein

Egg Beaters, 1 Cup = 24 g protein

Chicken, white meat, raw, without skin, 1 oz = 6.3 g protein

Chicken, dark meat, raw, without skin 1 oz = 5.6 grams protein

Beef, lean only, all grades, raw 1 oz = 5.9 grams protein

Ground beef, 90/10, raw 1 oz = 5.6 grams protein

Ground turkey, 85/15, raw, 1 oz = 4.8 grams protein

Turkey, white meat, raw, without skin 1 oz = 6.6 grams protein

Turkey, dark meat (thigh), raw, without skin 1 oz = 6 grams protein

Pork, fresh, lean, without skin, raw 1 oz = 6 grams protein

Tilapia, fresh, raw, filet 1 oz = 5.7 grams protein

Grouper, fish, mixed species, raw 1 oz = 5.5 grams protein

Cod, fish, Atlantic, raw 1 oz = 5 grams protein

Tuna fish, canned in water, drained, solids 1 oz = 5.5 grams protein

Haddock, fish, raw 1 oz = 4.6 grams protein

Halibut, fish, Greenland or North America, raw, 1 oz = 4 grams protein

Salmon, fish, Atlantic, raw 1 oz = 5.6 grams protein

Sea Bass, fish, mixed species, raw 1 oz = 5.2 grams protein

Cottage cheese, 1% milkfat 1 oz = 3.5 grams protein

Be careful how you prepare your proteins. They should never be fried, because this adds calories. During this program and over the long-term, I suggest baking, grilling, or broiling as ways to cook with variety. Keep in mind that marinating can also increase the amount of nutrient-poor calories and sodium. Do not season meat or fish with store-bought seasonings or marinades.

I recommend using a homemade product or a specialty product like Mrs. Dash (low sodium). Often spices can add variety and provide new flavor to proteins without adding calories or sodium.

Avoid breading proteins on this plan. Breading products contain a high amount of carbohydrates as well as sodium.

Fish is a very powerful protein source. Don't underestimate the power of fish. Although it is probably the toughest of the proteins to prepare, it is also the leanest of the bunch in terms of calories per weight and should be included in your diet if you choose to eat fish. Eating fish once per day will ensure that a variety of proteins and other nutrients are included in your diet.

If you are pregnant or worried about mercury, talk to your doctor; but recent studies have shown a decrease in concern over mercury concentrations in fish.[13]

All meats do contain cholesterol, but there is a difference between meat options in terms of amino acids, protein amounts, and fat content.

Dietary cholesterol and hereditary factors should be considered in a healthy diet. If you have been told by your doctor/dietitian that you have high HDL cholesterol, please talk to them before changing your diet. Meat can be incorporated into every healthy diet though. [14]

What kind of red meat should I eat?

Over the last 20 years, cholesterol has been a popular topic for the health-conscious American media. During the anti-cholesterol craze, beef was labeled as a high cholesterol food. Certain types of beef should be avoided for caloric reasons, and there are other types which can be included in a healthy way. Any ground beef with a ratio worse than 90% meat and 10% fat should be avoided to ensure a lean meat.

Rib eyes and prime ribs are examples of steaks that should be avoided. If the steak has a lot of marbling in the middle, it should be avoided for long-term consistency. Lean ground beef, sirloin steak, flank steak, and filet mignon are all lower in fat and high in protein. Do not be afraid to include these types of beef in your diet.

If you choose to eat beef, just keep in mind that with this program we are suggesting choices. Other meat options are completely safe as well.

What kind of turkey should I eat?

Be careful when choosing turkey. For the most part, turkey is a very healthy food. The food companies understand that when Americans see turkey, they think it's healthy. As a result, some businesses use low-cost foods and "healthy" labels to entice buyers to pay higher prices.

Turkey is a great example of this facade. You will notice ground turkey in the meat section at the grocery store. Beware of ground turkey that has high fat content, similar to ground beef. Look for light colored meat, often indicating breast meat, then make sure to read the label for fat content. I suggest a ground turkey of at least 85% lean with 15% fat (or less).

Deli meat turkey is also a reasonably healthy option, as far as fat and cholesterol are concerned. However, beware of the sodium content in deli meat. Just know that even at meat carving stations, they can show you nutrition labels.

Speak up for yourself and ask to see this information. If you choose to eat lunch meat, make sure you are eating low-sodium options.

What kind of chicken should I eat?

Chicken is considered similar to turkey in the sense that most Americans hear the word chicken and automatically think of something healthy. Chicken can be included in a healthy diet, but make sure you are eating chicken breast most of the time.

Just like turkey, dark meat is typically higher in fat; and that makes it a less healthy option in this program. To save time, canned chicken is also a good option, but be sure to vary canned with fresh to limit sodium intake.

What kind of pork should I eat?

Pork is a low-calorie protein when the right cuts are chosen and properly prepared. We suggest pork loin or chops because they are lower in fat. Bacon and sausage are not included in the protein option category for this plan, and we suggest you find alternatives to breakfast meats. To keep calories low, choose the leanest cuts of pork possible if you want to include pork in your diet.

Can I use dipping sauce?

If you must have a dipping sauce with your meat, use less than a tablespoon at each meal. An example of this would be A1 on steak and BBQ sauce on chicken. Be careful though, because even with these examples, A1 is high in sodium and BBQ sauce is high in sugar.

Using dipping sauces can easily increase a meal's sugar, carbohydrate, sodium, or calorie content. We recommend using lemon or lime juice, spices, and herbs to flavor foods.

Dietary Supplements, Shakes and Bars

Dietary supplements are defined as "a product taken orally that contains one or more ingredients that are intended to supplement one's diet and are not considered food." [15] Supplements, especially protein supplements, can enhance your fitness results.

Keep in mind that although some supplements may help your efforts to reach your fitness goals, consistency with your nutrition and exercise is the true key to your success. There are no miracles hiding on a supplement shelf. However, there are certainly supplements that will quickly make a difference in the way you look.

Supplement companies can put a variety of claims on the front of their labels because supplements aren't regulated by the FDA like other foods. However, they do have to be safe and list their ingredients and nutrient composition on the nutrition facts panel. When selecting a protein supplement, be sure to look for any ingredients that don't agree with your body. It is important to look at the amount of protein, calories, and added sugar per serving. Additionally, I suggest comparing supplements because both the cost and taste will vary from one brand to another.

Creatine

This supplement has been marketed for nearly 20 years now. Other than protein supplements, creatine is likely the most commonly used supplement on the planet. I believe creatine is an optimal supplement for a man who is just starting to work out. In short, creatine delivers extra water to the muscle cells, thereby allowing the muscle to work harder. Creatine has been known to cause some water retention as it delivers extra water to the muscles without having a little spillover under the skin. This water retention can be tolerated by a man who wants to build mass. However, most other individuals want to be as lean as possible, so any water retention would not be okay for them.

Therefore, if you're a male that is just getting started, creatine will help you get a good jump start. Just be careful with the dosages. Follow the recommended dose, and make sure you drink at least one gallon of water every day. It is very important to drink a lot of water when taking creatine. If an individual takes creatine but does not drink a lot of water, he may develop kidney problems.

Fat Burners

I never personally recommend this supplement, but some fat burners can be useful when taken properly. There are some fat burners that do exactly what they are supposed to do with little or no side effects. Other fat burners come with a set of risks that far outweigh the rewards. Some fat burners have side effects that include high blood pressure, heart arrhythmias, nausea, headaches and even death. If you choose to take a fat burner, please beware.

Omega Oils

When following a healthy diet, you will not be eating much fat in your food. You've probably heard before that the body needs some fat. Although it is true that the body needs some fat, that is not an excuse to go out and eat a pizza. The body needs good fat that is found in omega oils. Omega oils promote a host of benefits including better hair, skin and nails. However, the most important benefit of omega oils comes in the form of disease prevention. Omega oil helps prevent heart disease and high blood pressure. While our bodies need fat as an important source of energy, I suggest using omega oil. Omega oil has been shown to regulate satiety during weight loss and can aid in long-term weight management. [16]

Multivitamins

Vitamins can help you achieve your fitness goals. Most people can and should take a multivitamin on a daily basis. There are many brands with different health claims, but ultimately a vitamin should just be enhancing your diet. Most vitamins and minerals will be absorbed into the body when you have a varied diet. If there are certain foods you don't eat, or if you are concerned about having a vitamin deficiency of some sort, be sure to talk to your doctor. The best way to ensure you're properly nourishing your body would be to have your blood tested by a medical professional. I'm not saying this is necessary for everyone; but if you are worried, I recommend consulting a doctor before changing your diet.

Protein Shakes

Consuming protein shakes is imperative when it comes to eating healthy while living a busy lifestyle. They are an integral part of the Empty Your Bucket Nutrition Plan.

Protein shakes and bars are two of the most common supplements you will find today. However, some do not have the same level of bioavailability as others. Bioavailability in nutrition is defined as the "proportion of the nutrient that is digested, absorbed, and metabolized through normal pathways." [17]

Typically, proteins with lower bioavailability, such as soy protein and milk protein, cost less than other protein powders with higher bioavailability, such as whey and casein protein.

You will find quite a few brands of protein shakes on the market today containing more soy protein than they do whey protein. I know this can be challenging since all the protein shakes are found sitting on the same shelf at the store. Just remember to pick out the protein that is high in bioavailability. The best way to do this is by looking at the very first ingredient on the label. If the first ingredient does not contain the words whey or casein, you will know that the protein shake does not have a high bioavailability. I have noticed that a few supplement companies have gone as far as making the first ingredient on the label a blend of proteins, and you will see soy and milk protein along with whey and casein. The rule of thumb when looking at a blend is still the same: the first ingredient in the blend should be whey or casein.

Bioavailability also brings us back to the type of brand you choose. Unless you are avoiding dairy for personal, allergic, or religious reasons, choose a protein that is 100% whey or casein. These are the most effective proteins for the price and the most easily absorbed proteins, in my experience.[18] If you are lactose intolerant, choose a whey protein isolate which means all the lactose has been removed from the protein.

If you are gluten-free, make sure to choose a certified gluten-free protein because some facilities process other supplements that aren't gluten free, and cross contamination can occur. Some companies have been discovered using filler proteins that may be derived from wheat.

With a little planning, you can have a protein shake at just about any time or place. Best of all, protein shakes have come a long way from the old days of being a terrible tasting powder that requires a blender. There are many brands of protein shakes that taste very good and are easy to mix. Most only require water and a thermos or shaker. All you do is shake it up and you have a tasty—and more importantly—a complete meal while on the run.

There are hundreds—maybe even thousands—of protein shakes on the market today. Unfortunately, not all of them are good for you.

There are certain things you should look for when it comes to choosing a protein shake. When you consider that we recommend consuming protein shakes on a daily basis, it is very important that you understand how to find a healthy protein shake for you.

A large well-known supplement company stands to lose a lot of market share and confidence in their products if a test comes back showing the numbers on the label are false. Therefore, it is always a good idea to buy protein shakes from the only brand we endorse. A smaller, newer supplement company does not have as much to lose if their label claims come up false. They can simply change the name of their supplement company and quickly put the bogus product out once again. The moral of the story is to stick with my recommendations when it comes to any supplement.

Taste is also very important when it comes to your protein shakes. It is unrealistic to think that you are going to drink your protein shakes everyday if the shake doesn't taste good. Whey protein has a very mild taste that makes it quite palatable to your taste buds.

In a perfect world, every protein shake would taste like a milkshake. The good news is there are some protein shakes out there that come very close. The bad news is that some of those great tasting shakes contain a high amount of sugar. There are some good tasting shakes out there that are not filled with sugar. It's your job to find them.

The rule of thumb on sugar in protein shakes is to stay away from any shake that has a ratio of more than 1 gram of sugar for every 5 grams of protein. For example, a protein shake should contain no more than 4 grams of sugar for every 20 grams of protein (1:5). Once again, please be aware that many supplement companies assume you are naive. They think you'll be so thrilled with the taste that you will never check the sugar content. They get a lot of people this way. Those poor people drink their shakes every day and wonder why they aren't getting in shape.

Protein Bars

Protein bars should only be used when you can't get to a shake. A shake is healthier than a protein bar, but I understand that sometimes a shake is not a realistic option. Just keep in mind that protein bars often are made to mimic candy bars. Although these products may include some protein, they are often covered in chocolate or flavored with extra sugar.

If you have not had a protein bar in your life or in a while, I can tell you there are many good tasting protein bars on the market today. The problem with protein bars is, just like a protein shake, tasting good does not mean the protein bar is good for you. I would avoid protein bars altogether, unless it is your only choice.

Be sure to use the same guidelines mentioned above for protein shakes when choosing protein bars. Watch out for sugar. Check the first ingredient. Know what ingredients are in the product before you buy.

Portion Control

In a perfect world, I would like everyone to measure out the amount of carbohydrates they're eating with a food scale or measuring cups. However, I understand that most people are busy, so carrying around measuring cups to restaurants isn't suggested. With that in mind, I've come up with a convenient solution for time-consuming measurements.

A great and easy way to measure your food is by using hand measurements. Our hand is unique to each of us; therefore, you can use this hand measuring system:

A fist for starchy carbs
A palm for protein
A thumb for fats
Two fists for vegetables

Sweeteners

You may want to use a low-calorie sweetener such as Splenda, Truvia, stevia or other sugar substitute. Sugar substitutes are manufactured to be low or free of carbohydrates while still tasting sweet. Keep in mind that there is conflicting research on long-term health effects of sweeteners, so we suggest--as with all food groups--to use them in moderation. I suggest you try stevia or Truvia.

The 3 Keys to Your Success

1. Learn to Cook Efficiently

In today's world we have many options that help us save time. I believe there is a time and a place to be more efficient in your life. However, if you truly want to be lean and muscular, you should not cut corners when it comes to your nutrition. This includes making the sacrifice of cooking fresh, healthy meals on a consistent basis.

Over the years, when training clients, I've noticed trends in our fast-paced society. There are a lot of people who no longer wish to, or know how to, cook for themselves. Even if you think you're choosing healthy options or eating at "clean" restaurants, these places can never give you the results you're looking for over the long-term. Restaurants can be fun on occasion, and in a pinch, there are options that can fit your goals. However, you'll never know completely what is being put in your food. The only way to have complete control of your body is by knowing what you put into it.

Thankfully, there are a few simple things you can do to avoid spending long hours in the kitchen. For example, meal preparation is a growing trend right now. When you cook large amounts of meats and vegetables in bulk, it can help you save time when packing lunches all week. Just choose one day a week and set aside a few hours for this task. Then you can be sure that you'll have healthy eating options during the week. If you don't spend this time being proactive, you are much more likely to indulge in a last-minute fast food trip.

I also recommend not seasoning your food when meal prepping. Cook chicken breasts plain and then season them as you eat so one day you can have something that tastes different from what you ate the day before. Variety will help you keep life interesting.

Variety is a great tool but try not to get too elaborate with your meals. If you love to eat that way, then that's your choice. However, I believe that over time, that approach will become exhausting. Save big meals for when you want an extra treat or when you are having a celebration. Make food that you know you love and stick with the decisions you made during the meal planning process. In order to maintain this lifestyle over the long-term, you'll need to put life first. One great way to do that is to avoid feeling overwhelmed and to keep cooking as simple as possible.

2. Don't Skip Breakfast

I know I touched briefly on this area when talking about sleep, but I feel the need to address this area again because there is a significant problem today regarding breakfast. When you want to get healthy and get in shape, breakfast is the most important meal of the day. Unfortunately, most people don't eat breakfast.

Many people skip breakfast entirely, often using the excuse that they're simply not hungry.
The truth is—most often—individuals are too lazy in the morning to prepare breakfast.

Those who do eat breakfast can prepare something and eat it in just a few minutes. However, most of the breakfast foods people eat on the go are loaded with carbohydrates and devoid of protein. As a trainer and coach, I am always interested in what individuals eat for breakfast.

The most common response is something along the lines of cereal. Cereal is not healthy because it does not give your body a slow release of carbohydrates. Even wheat cereals won't cut it. Additionally, there is not enough protein in the milk to supply the amount of protein your body needs in the morning.

You must have real protein at breakfast, which means cooking steak, egg whites, etc. You will have to learn how to budget enough time in the morning to cook and eat your breakfast. I recommend that you try to create a multitasking routine at breakfast. I often find time to read scripture while my breakfast cooks on the stove. You can pack lunches for your family while you're making eggs.

Best of all, you will get better at preparing breakfast. It will become part of your daily routine. One last tip that can really help you save time in the morning is to have hard-boiled eggs ready to go. Hard-boiled eggs can help if you find yourself in a hurry. Remember, practicality always comes first when it comes to the kitchen, and it is the most important at breakfast.

3. Learn to Eyeball Measurements

When you are at the beginning of your journey—especially when changing your diet—it is helpful to weigh and measure your food. It only takes a few seconds, and these steps let you know that you're eating the right amount. Do you know what a five-ounce chicken breast looks like? Most likely you don't, because all your life you have not considered the size. The reality is that you do not need a ten-ounce chicken breast or a twelve-ounce steak.

If you are going to adopt the attitude of having four to seven ounces at each meal, it is essential that you learn to eyeball the right amounts. You may not want to weigh your meat each time you prepare a meal. Get practical and learn how to estimate the weight of meat.

Here are a few guidelines that will help you when learning measurements:

Tip of your thumb = about 1 teaspoon (this is a typical serving for fats)

Entire thumb = about 1 tablespoon (this is a typical serving for nut butters, dips, and dressings)

Cupped palm or index finger = about 1 oz (this is a typical cheese or nut serving size)

Closed fist = about one cup (this is a typical grain or fruit serving)

Open hand = about 3 to 4 oz (this is a typical meat serving, depending on thickness)

It will take some time to develop your accuracy for estimating food portions. This is completely normal. You can keep this task fun and simple by making it a game. This is a fantastic way to get kids on board. Again, take your time, and you'll get better at this skill as you practice it consistently.

Sample Meal Plans

Here are several sample meal plans you can use as a part of the Empty Your Bucket Plan. Feel free to use the ones right here in the book or take a picture of it with your phone. As you get used to this kind of healthy eating, not only will you feel great, you'll look great as well. If you would like to have a printable PDF of these, visit Emptyyourbucketplan.com.

DAY	Breakfast	Shake	Lunch	Shake	Dinner	Shake
MON	Three egg whites and stir fried veggies	12 to 16 oz of water for 2 scoops of protein	Grilled Chicken and salad	12 to 16 oz of water for 2 scoops of protein	Salmon and stir veggies and salad	6 to 8 oz of water with one 1 scoop of protein
TUE	Veggie omelet	12 to 16 oz of water for 2 scoops of protein	Zucchini noodles and steak	12 to 16 oz of water for 2 scoops of protein	Turkey burgers green beans	6 to 8 oz of water with one 1 scoop of protein
WED	Three egg whites and stir fried veggies	12 to 16 oz of water for 2 scoops of protein	Turkey burgers and guacamole	12 to 16 oz of water for 2 scoops of protein	Grilled chicken breast and kale salad	6 to 8 oz of water with one 1 scoop of protein
THU	Veggie omelet	12 to 16 oz of water for 2 scoops of protein	Rotisserie chicken and cauliflower rice	12 to 16 oz of water for 2 scoops of protein	Seared tuna and cesar salad	6 to 8 oz of water with one 1 scoop of protein
FRI	Three egg whites and stir fried veggies	12 to 16 oz of water for 2 scoops of protein	Turkey meat balls and green beans	12 to 16 oz of water for 2 scoops of protein	Salmon and cauliflower mash	6 to 8 oz of water with one 1 scoop of protein
SAT	Veggie omelet	12 to 16 oz of water for 2 scoops of protein	Tuna salad with 3 boiled eggs	12 to 16 oz of water for 2 scoops of protein	Asparagus and turkey loaf	6 to 8 oz of water with one 1 scoop of protein
SUN	Three egg whites and stir fried veggies	12 to 16 oz of water for 2 scoops of protein	Chicken cutlet with zucchini noodles	12 to 16 oz of water for 2 scoops of protein	Lean burger patties and broccoli	6 to 8 oz of water with one 1 scoop of protein

NAME: START DATE:

The Empty Your Bucket Plan

Empty Your Bucket Plan
SUSTAINABLE LIFE TRANSFORMATIONS

DAY	Breakfast	Shake	Lunch	Shake	Dinner	Shake
MON	4 boiled egg with half avocado	12 to 16 oz of water for 2 scoops of protein	Grilled chicken with asparagus and one handful of brown rice	12 to 16 oz of water for 2 scoops of protein	Salmon and spinach	6 to 8 oz of water with one 1 scoop of protein
TUE	3 to 4 egg omelet with stir fried veggies and half cup of oatmeal	12 to 16 oz of water for 2 scoops of protein	Ground turkey and Brocoli	12 to 16 oz of water for 2 scoops of protein	Tuna fish with one teaspoon of mayo with salad	6 to 8 oz of water with one 1 scoop of protein
WED	6 oz of sirloin steak and two egg whites	12 to 16 oz of water for 2 scoops of protein	Turkey burgers, cesar salad (No croutons) and quinoa	12 to 16 oz of water for 2 scoops of protein	Mahi and stir fried veggies	6 to 8 oz of water with one 1 scoop of protein
THU	Ground turkey, two scrambled eggs and two slices of Ezekiel bread	12 to 16 oz of water for 2 scoops of protein	Grilled chicken thighs with green beans	12 to 16 oz of water for 2 scoops of protein	Salmon and asparagus	6 to 8 oz of water with one 1 scoop of protein
FRI	4 egg omelet with one tomato, seasoned with Mrs. Dash	12 to 16 oz of water for 2 scoops of protein	Grilled chicken breast, asparagus, and one handful of couscous	12 to 16 oz of water for 2 scoops of protein	Grilled chicken thighs and cesar salad (No croutons)	6 to 8 oz of water with one 1 scoop of protein
SAT	Salmon and two scrambled eggs with one handful brown rice	12 to 16 oz of water for 2 scoops of protein	8 oz of sirloin steak and tossed salad	12 to 16 oz of water for 2 scoops of protein	Green beans and ground turkey	6 to 8 oz of water with one 1 scoop of protein
SUN	Turkey bacon and two eggs over easy	12 to 16 oz of water for 2 scoops of protein	Ground turkey with broccoli and half sweet potato.	12 to 16 oz of water for 2 scoops of protein	Mashed cauliflower and Lemon pepper chicken	6 to 8 oz of water with one 1 scoop of protein

NAME: START DATE:

Empty Your Bucket Plan
SUSTAINABLE LIFE TRANSFORMATIONS

DAY	Breakfast	Shake	Lunch	Shake	Dinner	Shake
MON	Three egg whites and stir fried veggies with two slices of Ezekiel bread	12 to 16 oz of water with one 2 scoop of protein	Chicken, and salad	12 to 16 oz of water with one 2 scoop of protein	Salmon and stir veggies and salad	6 to 8 oz of water with one 1 scoop of protein
TUE	Veggie omelet	12 to 16 oz of water with one 2 scoop of protein	Zucchini noodles, steak and on cup of brown rice	12 to 16 oz of water with one 2 scoop of protein	Turkey burgers green beans	6 to 8 oz of water with one 1 scoop of protein
WED	Three egg whites and stir fried veggies	12 to 16 oz of water with one 2 scoop of protein	Turkey burgers and guacamole	12 to 16 oz of water with one 2 scoop of protein	Grilled chicken breast and kale salad	6 to 8 oz of water with one 1 scoop of protein
THU	Veggie omelet and half cup oatmeal	12 to 16 oz of water with one 2 scoop of protein	Rotisserie chicken and cauliflower rice	12 to 16 oz of water with one 2 scoop of protein	Seared tuna and cesar salad	6 to 8 oz of water with one 1 scoop of protein
FRI	Three egg whites and half cup of oatmeal	12 to 16 oz of water with one 2 scoop of protein	Turkey meat balls and green beans	12 to 16 oz of water with one 2 scoop of protein	Salmon and cauliflower mash	6 to 8 oz of water with one 1 scoop of protein
SAT	Veggie omelet	12 to 16 oz of water with one 2 scoop of protein	Tuna salad with 3 boiled eggs and couscous	12 to 16 oz of water with one 2 scoop of protein	Asparagus and turkey loaf	6 to 8 oz of water with one 1 scoop of protein
SUN	Three egg whites and stir fried veggies	12 to 16 oz of water with one 2 scoop of protein	Chicken cutlet with zucchini noodles	12 to 16 oz of water with one 2 scoop of protein	Lean burger patties and broccoli	6 to 8 oz of water with one 1 scoop of protein

NAME: START DATE:

Chapter 7
The Role of Hydration in the Body

It is important to note that proper hydration plays a big role in the way a person looks.[19] Not being properly hydrated can actually make a lean body look somewhat bloated or even overweight. To understand how hydration plays a key role in how you look, you need to understand a little about how the body works.

Our bodies are designed to take care of themselves. We know that when a body is dehydrated, it stores more water to protect itself, causing bloating. This can make a lean body appear larger than it is and misleading for fitness goals. It's imperative that you stay properly hydrated if you want to look and feel your best. Proper hydration can help your body perform and feel it's best.

I suggest drinking between 3/4 gallon to one gallon of pure water each day. Some low-calorie sweetened water beverages are okay, but just keep in mind that these should only be used as occasional treats. Remember to always read the labels because sometimes claims such as "no added sugar" means there are still added calories in beverages. These products should be avoided. Drinking calories is not a good choice for long-term weight goals.

For example, one can of soda can have the same number of calories as a protein shake or a piece of fruit without any of the health benefits.

Again, our bodies are designed to take care of themselves. Your body knows when you are properly hydrated and when you are not. When the body feels dehydrated, it stores more water to protect itself. For example, if you do not drink enough water on a daily basis, your body will start to hold water as a way to protect itself from dehydration. This can be disastrous to your fitness goals. Your body will hide the muscle tone you work so hard for. It is imperative that you stay properly hydrated if you want to look your best.

If you are going to drink enough fluids to stay properly hydrated, I suggest investing in a water filter for your house. You can buy a filter for your sink or a water pitcher that has a filter built into it. If you buy all your water bottled, you will spend a small fortune on water when you drink ¾ of a gallon to one gallon a day.

Sports Drinks

Do not be fooled by all the advertising regarding so-called "healthy" drinks that promise energy for workouts or replenishment after a workout. These drinks rehydrate and restore sugars lost during extreme workouts. By extreme I mean long periods of time without food or drink.

A gym workout or even a 5K run doesn't count. Your body can replenish itself with the food and drink you give it before and after your workout. Do not let yourself fall prey to the unbelievable amount of sugar in "healthy" sports drinks.

Alcoholic Beverages

I know that some adults like to drink alcohol. It is important to keep drinking in moderation. But what exactly does that mean? According to Mayo Clinic, moderate alcohol use means up to one drink a day for women of all ages and men older than age 65, and up to two drinks a day for men age 65 and younger.

Examples of one drink include:

- **Beer:** 12 fluid ounces (355 milliliters)
- **Wine:** 5 fluid ounces (148 milliliters)
- **Distilled spirits (80 proof):** 1.5 fluid ounces (44 milliliters) [20]

If at any point you are drinking as a way to handle stress or avoid certain situations, please stop drinking and talk to a medical professional. As you know from my personal story, substance abuse and depression can lead to very serious consequences.

If you decide to drink alcohol, please know that it will slow the progress of your fitness results. But the biggest lesson is that everything should be in moderation. Here are a few tips you need to know that makes drinking alcohol less harmful to your fitness goals.

First, do not mix your alcohol with something caloric. This includes regular sodas, fruit juices, or mixers. If a drink has many ingredients that often means just more flavorings and "fun" additions instead of more alcohol. Typical pitfalls to avoid are Long Island Iced Tea, Margarita, and Daiquiri-type drinks. Instead, substitute a dash of lime or lemon, diet soda, or even a non-sugary beverage. This small change will drastically limit the damage to your fitness efforts.

I also recommend staying away from beer and wine. These drinks are high in carbohydrates, sugars and calories. These are also lower in alcohol content than other drinks, so people may drink more to feel the same effect. Instead, stick to clear alcohol like vodka and clear rum.

Mix these drinks with diet additives or club soda and a splash of citrus to be equally refreshed but to keep your fitness and diet goals on track.

Another common pitfall that comes with drinking is that it lowers your inhibitions and makes you less responsible. This includes the food that you eat while drinking alcohol. Individuals who are fit and practice consistency and moderation in their diet know that alcohol is already a splurge in calories.

As mentioned above, there are ways to reduce the caloric intake with alcohol, but if you finish the night with a large snack or even eat food while drinking, you can sabotage your healthy diet. Try to be sensible when you eat while drinking. Do not let your guard down. The best way to combat a hangover is drinking plenty of water and having a plan for food after a night out. [21] Have a sandwich ready or another light snack to avoid a late-night fast food trip. Again, be intentional and responsible with alcohol and try to keep in mind that drinking slows down your progress toward your fitness goals and really clouds your mind, even a couple of days after.

Chapter 8
Exercise

While diet is essential in helping you look and feel better, exercise plays a critical role in your physical fitness. I prefer two specific forms of exercise. First and foremost, I love High Intensity Interval Training (HIIT) cardio. In addition to HIIT cardio, I also recommend Slow-burn cardio as a great way to lose weight.

High Intensity Interval Training (HIIT) Cardio

When most people think of cardio, they think of long, boring jogs, or endless hours on the elliptical.

I've got some good news for you: this method of cardio is not boring at all. In fact, it takes less time than you'd expect and is far superior to traditional cardio.

HIIT cardio alternates between high-intensity and low-intensity exercise. For example, a participant may sprint for 30 seconds and then walk for 60 seconds. HIIT can even be used both anaerobically in the gym with weights and aerobically with cardio.

Here are three specific reasons why I love HIIT cardio.

HIIT cardio is very efficient.

HIIT is very time-efficient, even with our busy schedules. Circuit training workouts are only thirty to forty-five minutes long. The intensity of HIIT demands such short workouts instead of participation in long, often boring workouts that can take anywhere from one to two hours. Those less-intense workouts often yield poor results by comparison with HIIT in terms of weight loss.

Clear cardiovascular benefits.

HIIT workouts not only increase one's aerobic capacity, they also increase one's anaerobic capacity. By comparison, jogging alone only increases one's aerobic capacity, not one's anaerobic capacity. Interestingly, a recent study indicated a 14 percent increase in aerobic capacity from six weeks of HIIT, whereas six weeks of jogging alone in the same study provided only a 9 percent increase in aerobic capacity. More importantly, the same study showed virtually no improvement in one's anaerobic capacity from jogging alone, while HIIT provided an incredible 28 percent improvement in one's anaerobic capacity.

HIIT Cardio burns fat and builds muscle.

HIIT workouts boost your metabolism levels and help you burn more fat and calories when compared to steady-state aerobic activity such as running or cycling.

Intense workouts increase your body's rate of metabolism, such that it may remain increased hours after your exercise. This effect is known as the "afterburn effect" which follows intense workouts.

According to the *Journal of Applied Physiology*, women demonstrated a 30 percent increase in fat oxidation (a key indicator in fat loss) after performing seven HIIT workouts over a two-week period. HIIT also triggers human growth hormone (HGH), which is a key component for building muscle.

Slow-burn Cardio

In order to become fit, lower your BMI and reduce weight, one of the best-kept secrets in fitness is slow burn cardio. We recommend it at least three times a week. Experts recommend pairing this up with resistance training and targeting major muscle groups such as arms, legs, back and glutes. Resistance training helps burn more calories, lower BMI and build muscle.

BMI is an abbreviation for body mass index. This ratio represents your weight with respect to your height. It helps determine which category you fall in: underweight, overweight, obesity level 1, obesity level 2, obesity level 3 and normal weight. When you lower your BMI, it means you are also lowering your body weight.

When you want to lower your BMI and lose weight quickly, aerobic activity is the way to go. If cardio is a new experience for you, it is recommended that you start with consistent but low-impact activity, such as elliptical machine or brisk walking. As you adjust to this kind of workout, you can gradually increase the level of intensity.

After a few minutes of slow-paced cardio, your body bypasses the carbs and goes over to utilizing fat stores to avail energy. The fat burning stage usually starts after about 25 minutes of consistent slow-paced cardio. However, it is different in everyone owing to multiple factors. Technically, when you work harder and perform intense exercises, your heart rate shoots up and your body utilizes energy which is available quicker, and this is carbohydrates. With a lower heart rate, your body likes to fuel activity by using fat stored in the body.

The best way to participate in slow-burn cardio is through using a treadmill or stationary bike. You should walk on the treadmill for 45 minutes, ideally 1 hour; or ride on the stationary bicycle for 60 minutes at pretty much the same pace.

Here's an important tip: you can potentially triple your results if you do slow-burn cardio on an empty stomach.

Here are a few simple steps to get you going with slow-burn cardio. First, buy a Polar heart rate monitor to get the most accurate heart rate.

Next, you need to learn how to calculate your heart rate. There is a low heart rate range and a high heart rate range.

220 - age x .060 = your low heart rate range.

220 - age x .070 = your high heart rate range.

When you work out, you should stay in the range between these two heart rates for 45 minutes, ideally one hour. Again, for maximum results I recommend exercising on an empty stomach. If you have any medical concerns, please do not hesitate to consult with your doctor.

Chapter 9
Adapting to Your Environment

Life can be challenging at times. Things pop up and seem to throw a wrench in our daily, weekly or monthly plans. After training clients for years, I have seen a trend between the successful fitness people and the unsuccessful people.

I'm sure you've heard the saying, "When the going gets tough, the tough get going." This statement is very true when it comes to personal fitness. The people who succeed have the same tough lives as the people who don't succeed. The only difference is that the successful ones never let things get in their way. The successful adapt to their environment whereas the unsuccessful let their environment run their lives.

I believe in many cases unsuccessful people are subconsciously looking for reasons not to exercise and eat properly.

Here's an example regarding exercise: an unsuccessful client will tell us that they have to cancel their training session because they have a dentist appointment scheduled on the same day and time as their training appointment.

They'll tell us that they'll see us at their next scheduled training session without ever asking to make up the missed session. The successful client may have the same problem where their dentist appointment is scheduled at the same time as their training session, but the difference is they will ask to reschedule their training session to make it up. They understand their week might not go as planned and they adapt to make sure they get all their workouts in. They don't look for excuses not to exercise; they overcome the excuses.

Even more prevalent is the way clients make excuses about not eating properly. For example, the unsuccessful person will tell us that they couldn't eat a healthy lunch because they had a company lunch where a vendor brought in unhealthy options. Keep in mind, the unsuccessful client knew this lunch was coming for weeks. He knew there was a possibility that there may not be healthy options available.

The successful client will pack a healthy lunch for that day just in case there are no healthy options. Once again, the successful client adapted to their environment whereas the unsuccessful let their environment run their life.

Weekends are the most important time to adapt to your environment. For the most part, the weekdays have a routine to them. The weekends have no routine. One weekend you may be going to a wedding, and the next weekend you may have company in town. I can tell you that no matter what successful clients are doing on the weekend, they plan around it to ensure they exercise and eat properly. The unsuccessful client will tell us they couldn't exercise because they had company in town.

Additionally, they will tell us they couldn't eat healthy because their visitors don't like healthy food. These are just excuses, so they can rationalize not doing the right things in their mind.

The bottom line is that learning how to plan around things that pop up will allow you to become successful in your fitness goals. Do not find excuses to not exercise and eat properly.

You will be able to find an excuse just about every day. If you think that a very fit person doesn't have things come up in their lives just like you, you are mistaken. It's the way people adapt to their environment that separates the successful from the unsuccessful.

The next time you have a wrench thrown in your plans, do not let it throw you off track. Find a way to get around it while still maintaining your exercise and nutrition. That's how successful people live their lives, and that's how you should too.

Conclusion

This book was written to serve others. I genuinely believe that once we are physically, mentally and spiritually healthy, we can serve the Lord best. I would like to leave you with this final encouragement from the apostle Paul in 1 Timothy 4:7-9 (ESV):

"Have nothing to do with irreverent, silly myths. Rather train yourself for godliness; for while bodily training is of some value, godliness is of value in every way, as it holds promise for the present life and also for the life to come. The saying is trustworthy and deserving of full acceptance."

In these verses, the apostle Paul places things in order of importance: godliness is the true goal. This idea has fueled me and served as the inspiration for this book. I believe that how we do anything is how we do everything. If we can discipline ourselves to honor the temple of the Holy Spirit through proper nutrition and physical exercise, we can later translate those disciplines into our spiritual life.

We have an opportunity to make our lives a masterpiece that brings honor to our Lord and Savior Jesus Christ.

I hope that our connection does not end here.
If you would like to be added to our mailing list or if you are interested in further guidance, please feel free to contact me via email at emptyyourbucketplan@gmail.com or visit me on the web at www.Emptyyourbucketplan.com

About the Author

J.T. Tapias lives in Tampa, Florida, with his wife Ana Maria and his two daughters, Saramia and Hannah.

J.T. earned a B.S. in Counseling, and he's currently pursuing a Master's in substance abuse and eating disorders. J.T. holds multiple certifications in fitness and personal training, nutrition, and life coaching.

Among his accreditations are ACE, IFPA, NASM, IPEC Certified Professional Life Coach (with specialization in health and wellness), as well as being a Certified Health Counselor.

J.T. Tapias was born in Medellin, Colombia. He was raised in Brooklyn, New York, and learned from an early age that living a fit and healthy life was more of a lifestyle necessity than a now-and-again pastime. He started practicing martial arts at age five and continued until age twelve, at which point, his mother realized that if he didn't shift his focus to another sport, all her household goods would be destroyed. Soccer became his new passion. His rapid achievements in soccer led to the start of a professional career at age seventeen.

J.T. then spent a significant portion of his life playing soccer for teams in Europe and Latin America. U.S. Fitness and modeling were his next targets, and achievements soon followed.

He then created his own successful fitness brand and company. Equipped with ambition and pure drive, J.T. Tapias has utilized his fitness expertise to become a go-to guy for television networks including FitTV and the Travel Channel.

J.T. continues to advance and refine his training model to provide his clients with the best opportunity to gain and keep a healthy mind, body and spirit. According to J.T., "There's not a body without a mind or a mind without a body; and to be a victorious person, you need alignment through the Holy Spirit. All three components work together in direct correlation and harmony. Many trainers focus too much on the physical aspect of health and ignore the mind and the spirit. It is critical to recognize what is keeping your client from following a diet program or showing up for a scheduled session.

References

1. "Overweight and Obesity Statistics." *National Institute of Diabetes and Digestive and Kidney Diseases*, https://www.niddk.nih.gov/health-information/health-statistics/overweight-obesity

2. Horwich, Tamara B, et al. "The Relationship Between Obesity and Mortality in Patients with Heart Failure." *Journal of American College of Cardiology*, vol. 38, issue 3, pp. 789-795, https://www.sciencedirect.com/science/article/pii/S0735109701014486

3. "Carbohydrates." *Harvard School of Public Health*, USDA, www.hsph.harvard.edu/nutritionsource/carbohydrates/.

4. *Institute of Medicine, Dietary Reference Intakes for Energy, Carbohydrate, Fiber, Fat, Fatty Acids, Cholesterol, Protein, and Amino Acids (Macronutrients). 2005, National Academies Press: Washington, DC.*

5. Wu, T., et al. "Long-Term Effectiveness of Diet-plus-Exercise Interventions vs. Diet-Only Interventions for Weight Loss: a Meta-Analysis." *Obesity Reviews*, Blackwell Publishing Ltd, 19 Jan. 2009, onlinelibrary.wiley.com/doi/10.1111/j.1467-789X.2008.00547.x/full.

6. "Glycemic Index and Glycemic Load for 100+ Foods." *Harvard Health*

Publications, WebMD, Feb. 2015, www.health.harvard.edu/diseases-and-conditions/glycemic-index-and-glycemic-load-for-100foods

7. Fuller, Stacey, et al. "New Horizons for the Study of Dietary Fiber and Health: A Review."SpringerLink, Springer US, Feb. 2016, link.springer.com/article/10.1007/s11130-016-0529-6

8. "How to Use the Glycemic Index." What Is the Glycemic Index?, WebMD, www.webmd.com/diabetes/guide/glycemic-index-good-versus-bad-carbs#1.

9. Food Composition Databases Show Foods -- Brussels Sprouts, Raw, USDA, ndb.nal.usda.gov/ndb/foods/show/2879?manu=&fgcd=&ds=.

10. Food Composition Databases Show Foods -- Snacks, Trail Mix, Regular, USDA, ndb.nal.usda.gov/ndb/foods/show/6097?manu.

11. Dideriksen, Kasper, et al. "Influence of Amino Acids, Dietary Protein, and Physical Activity on Muscle Mass Development in Humans." *Nutrients - Human Nutrition Journal*, vol. 5, no. 3, 2013, pp. 852–876., doi:10.3390/nu5030852.

12. Aller, E E J G; Larsen, T M; Claus, H; Lindroos, A K; Kafatos, A; et al. International Journal of Obesity; London38.12 (Dec 2014): 1511-7.

13. Birch, Rebecca Jeffries, et al. "Trends in

Blood Mercury Concentrations and Fish Consumption among U.S. Women of Reproductive Age, NHANES, 1999-2010. *Environmental Research*, vol. 133, Aug. 2014, pp. 431–438. *Science Direct*, doi:10.1016/j.envres.2014.02.001.

14. Scientific Report of the 2015 Dietary Guidelines Advisory Committee - Advisory Report to the Secretary of Health and Human Services and the Secretary of Agriculture, pp. 1-571.

15. "Dietary Supplement." Merriam-Webster, www.merriam-webster.com/dictionary/dietarysupplement.

16. Parra, Dolores, et al. "A Diet Rich in Long Chain Omega-3 Fatty Acids Modulates Satiety in Overweight and Obese Volunteers during Weight Loss." *Appetite*, vol. 51, no. 3, Nov. 2008, pp. 676–680. *Science Direct*, doi:10.1016/j.appet.2008.06.003.

17. Srinivasan, V. Srini. "Bioavailability of Nutrients: A Practical Approach to In Vitro Demonstration of the Availability of Nutrients in Multivitamin-Mineral Combination Products." *The Journal of Nutrition*, vol. 131, no. 4, Apr. 2001, pp. 1349S–1350S., jn.nutrition.org/content/131/4/1349S.long.

18. Devries, M. C. and Phillips, S. M. (2015), Supplemental Protein in Support of Muscle Mass and Health: Advantage

Whey. Journal of Food Science, 80: A8–A15. doi:10.1111/1750-3841.12802

19. Katherine Zeratsky RD, LD. "Poor Hydration Associated with Higher BMI." *Mayo Clinic*, Mayo Foundation for Medical Education and Research, July 2016, www.mayoclinic.org/healthy-lifestyle/nutrition-and-healthy-eating/expert-blog/poor-hydration-associated-with-higher-bmi/bgp-20228129.

20. "Alcohol: If You Drink, Keep It Moderate." *Mayo Clinic*, https://www.mayoclinic.org/healthy-lifestyle/nutrition-and-healthy-eating/in-depth/alcohol/art-20044551

21. Tipple, Celeste T, et al. "A Review of the Physiological Factors Associated with Alcohol Hangover." *Current Drug Abuse Reviews*, vol. 9, no. 2, Aug. 2016, pp. 93–98. *Bentham Science Publishers*.

Made in the USA
Monee, IL
10 April 2023

31633542R00092